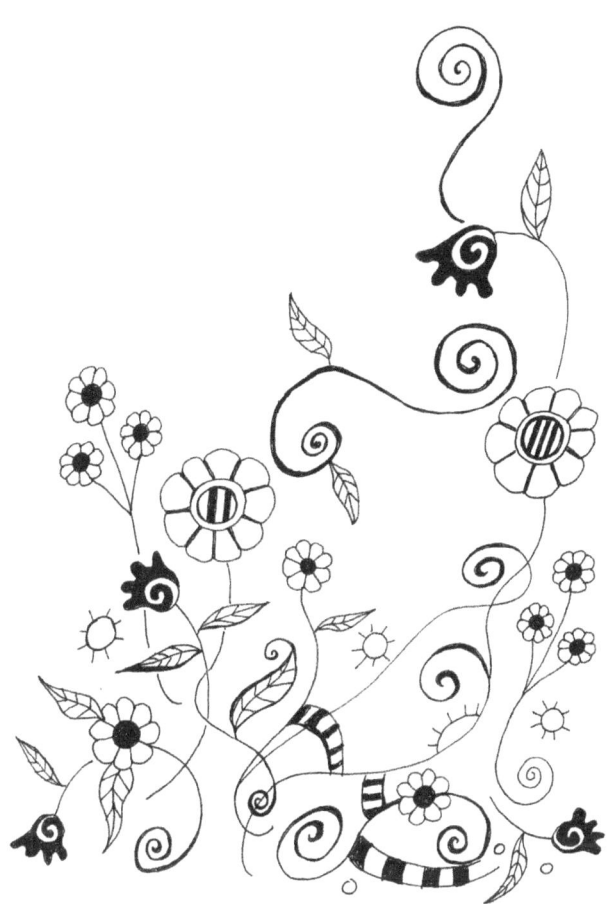

Strange Designs

drawings by

Kimberly Garvey

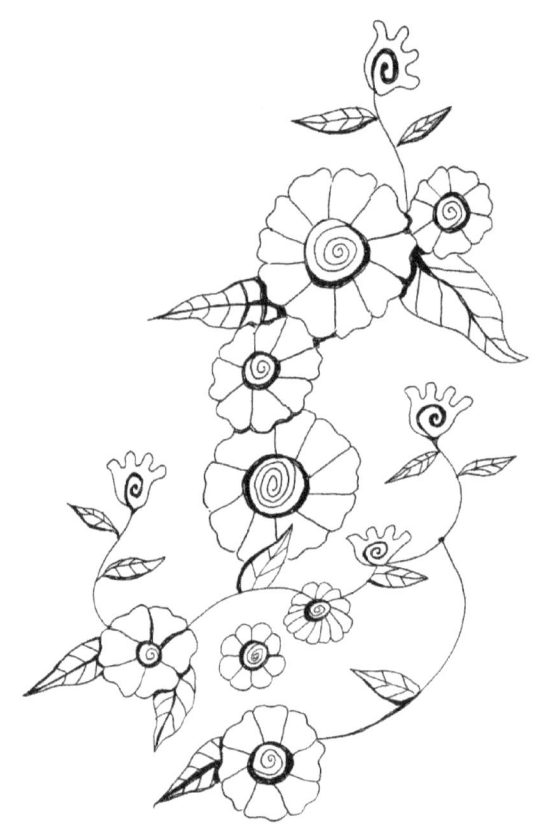

Kimberlygarvey.com

This book is dedicated to all of my friends and family who have encouraged and inspired me along the way.

Please note, if using markers you should put a piece of paper between the pages to prevent bleed-through.

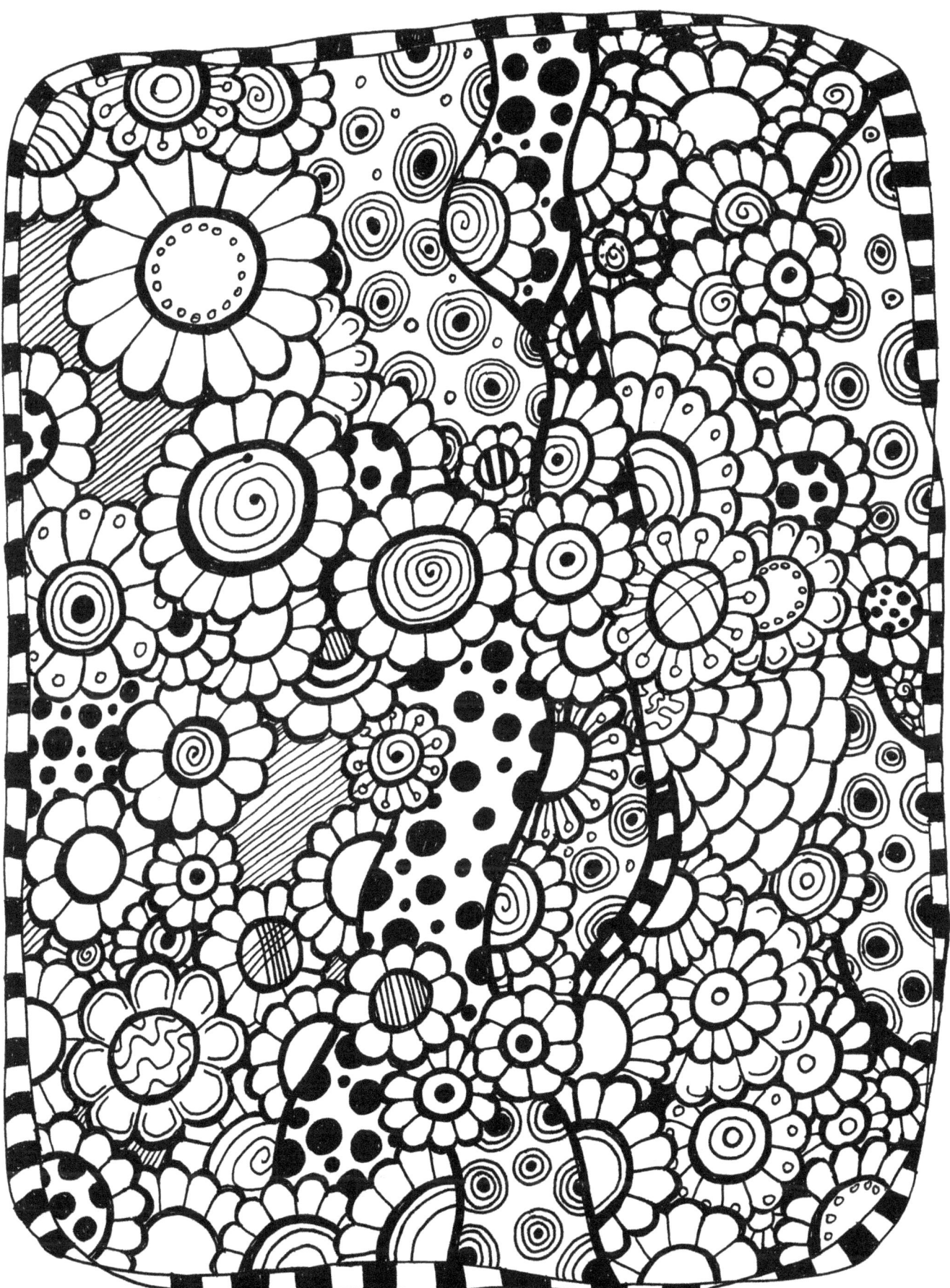

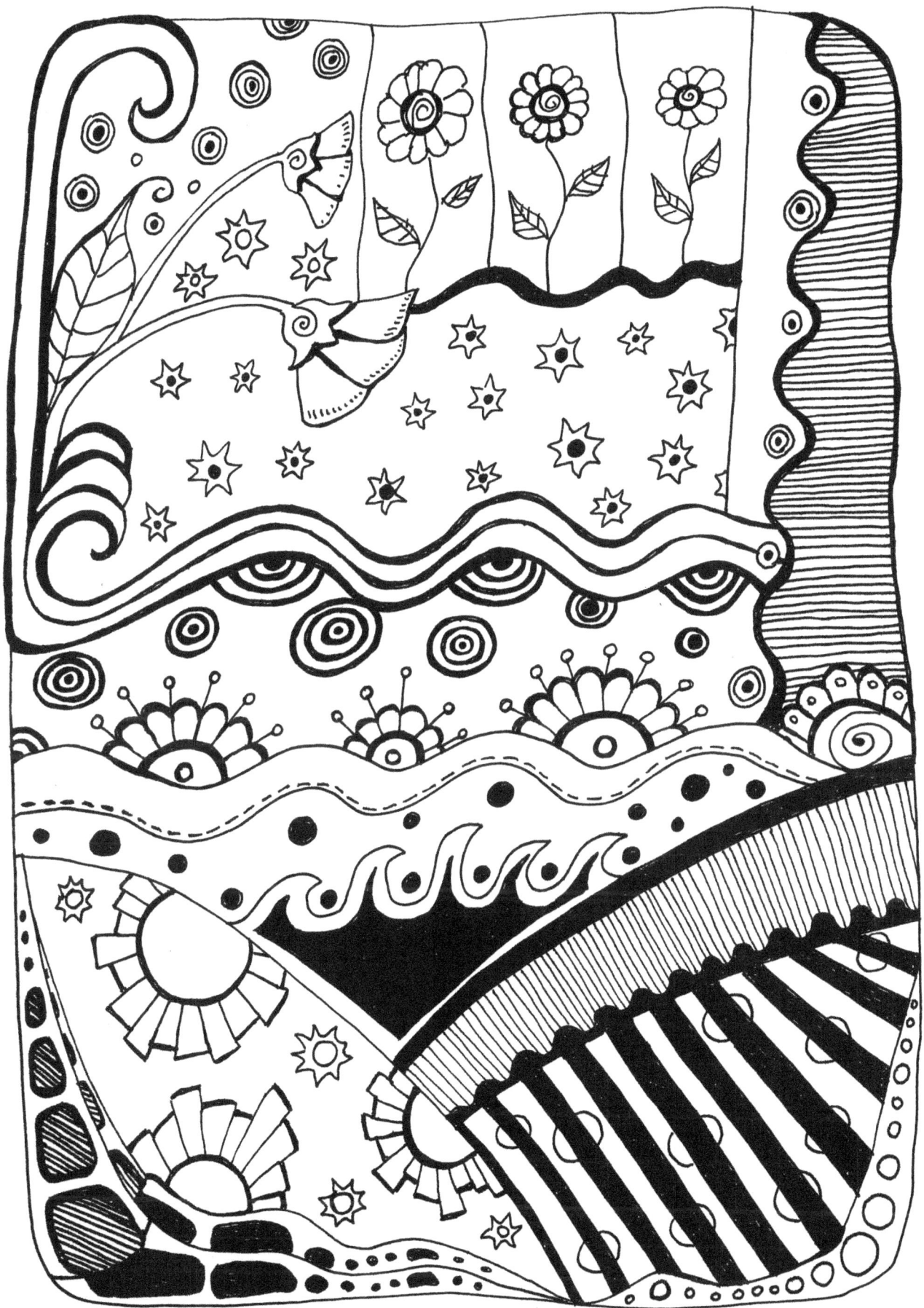

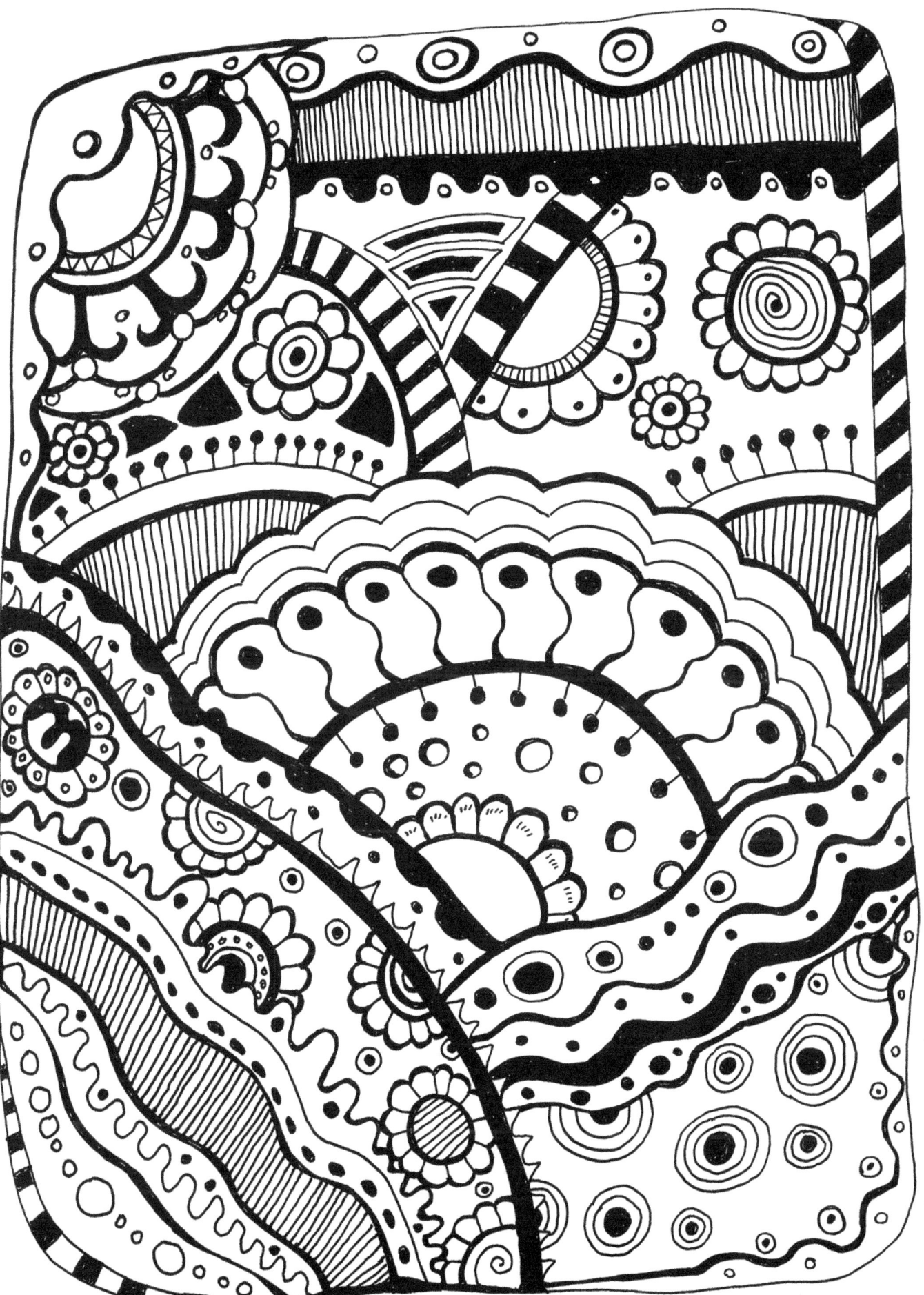

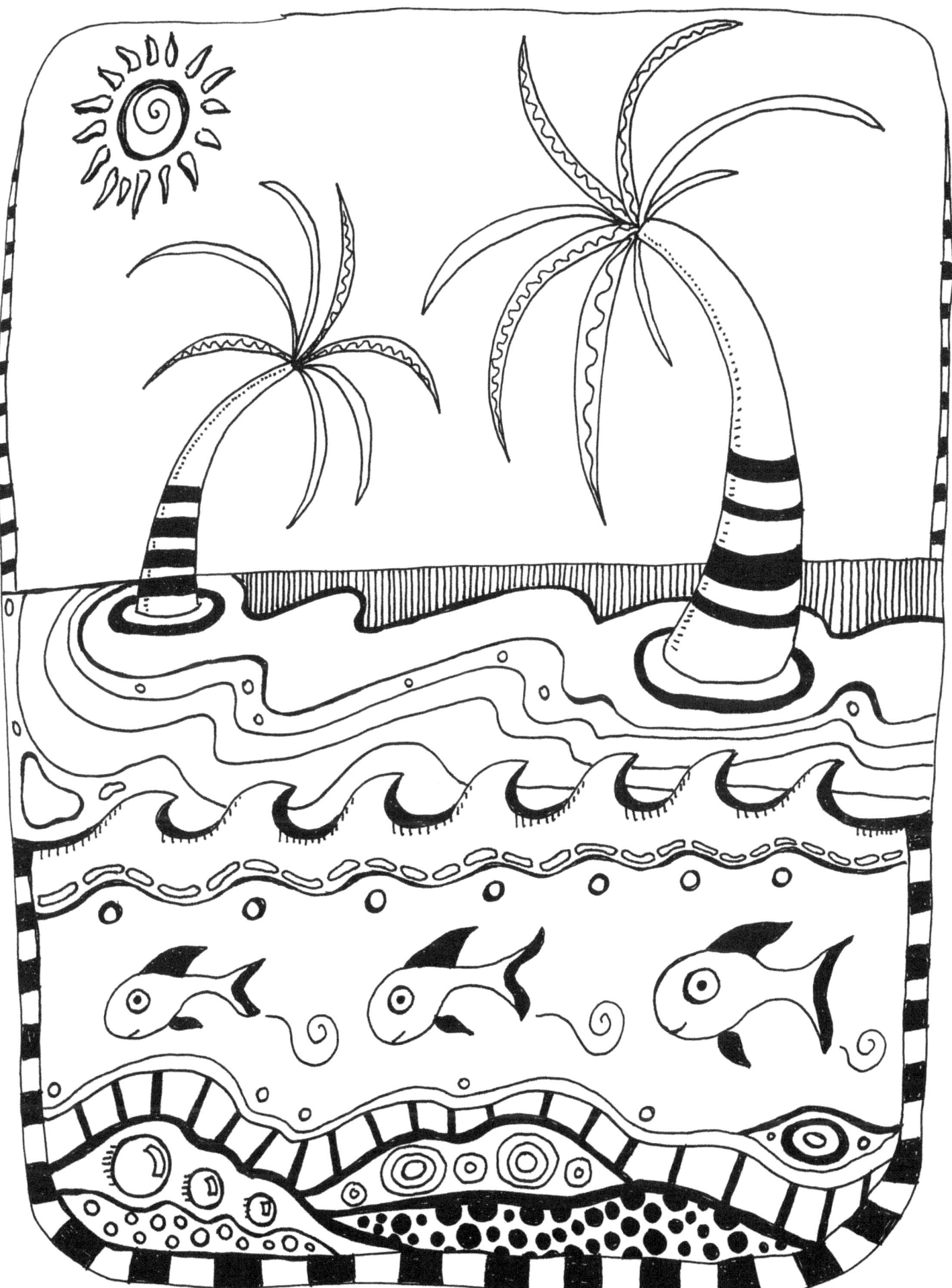

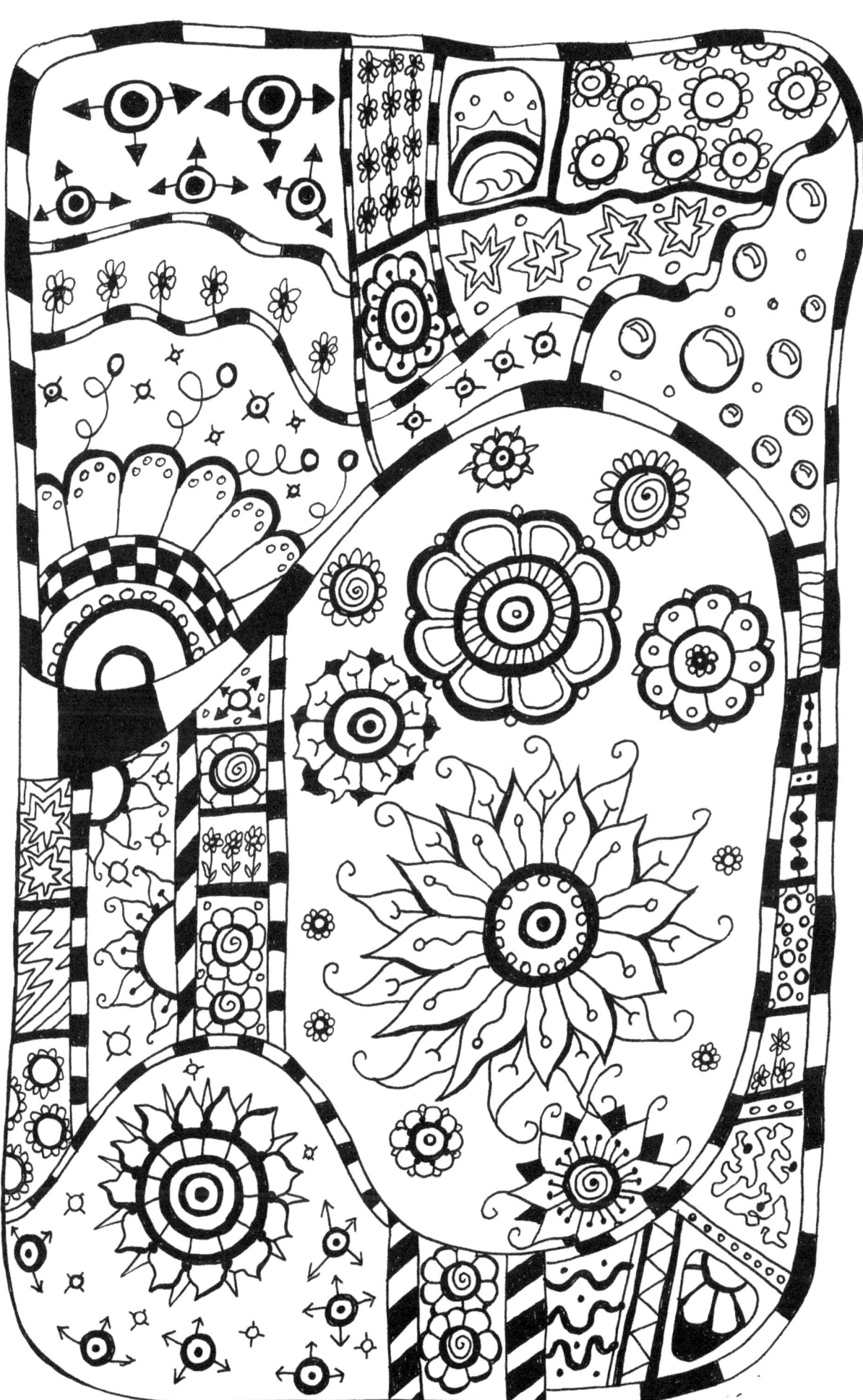

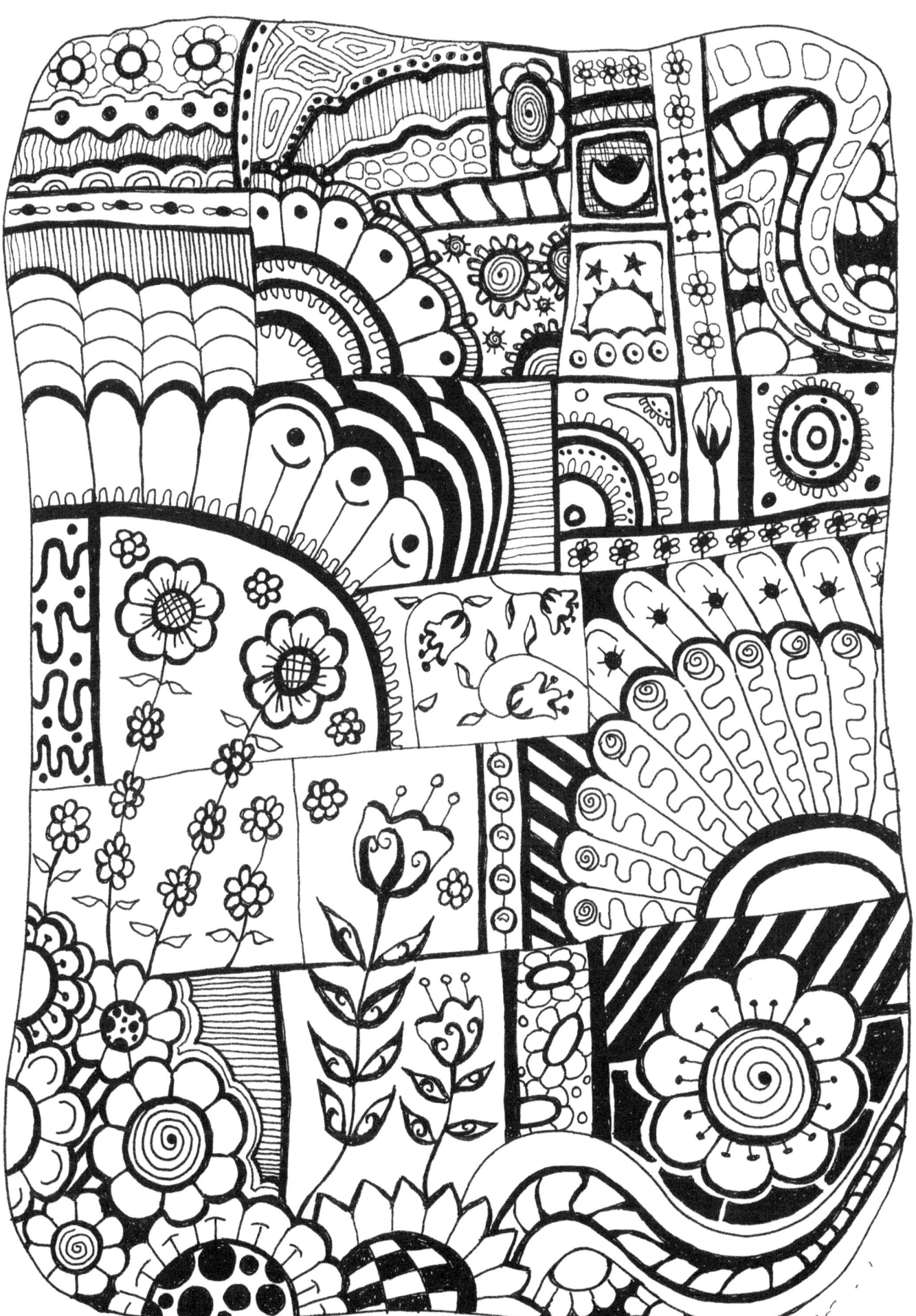

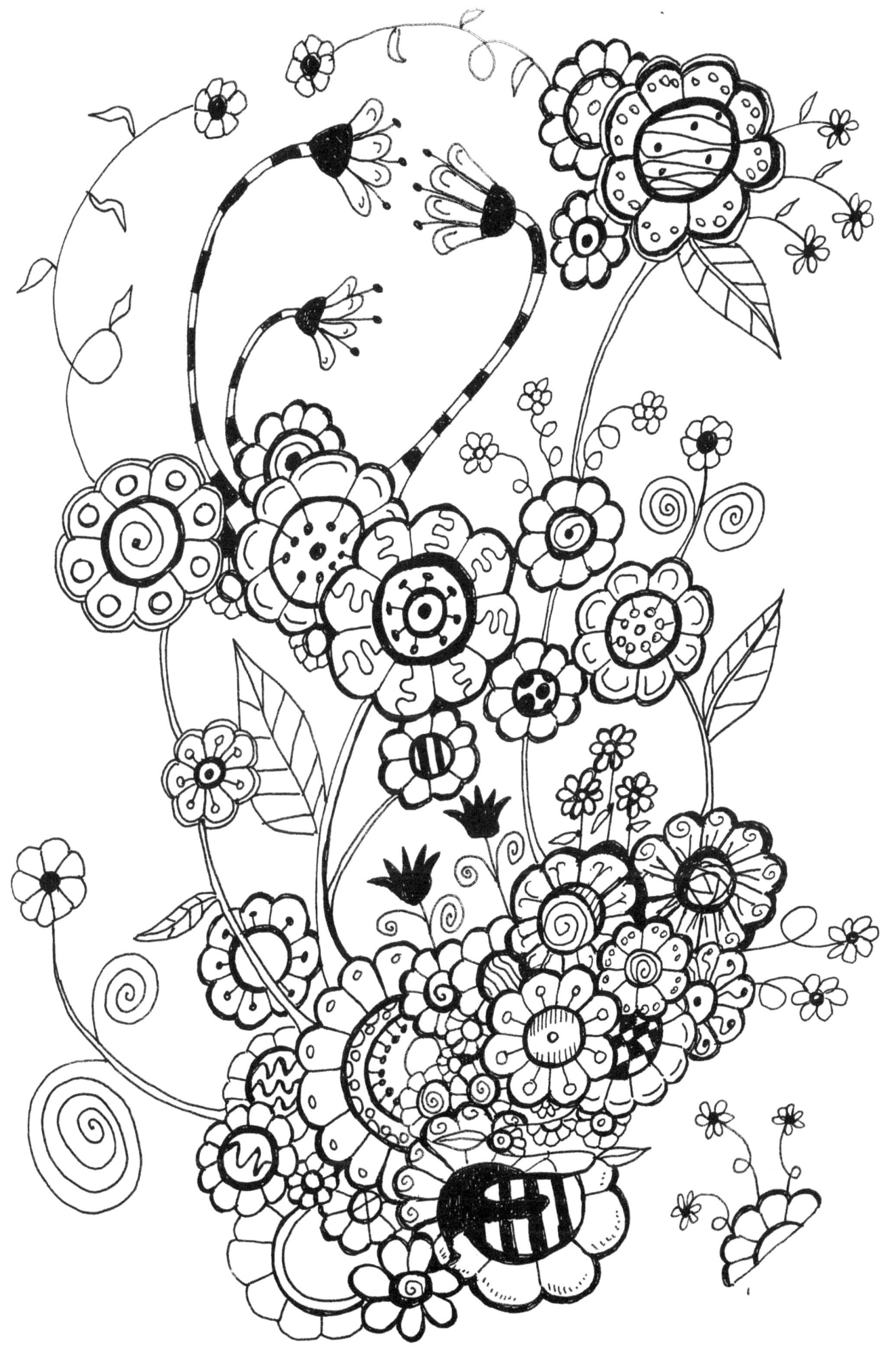

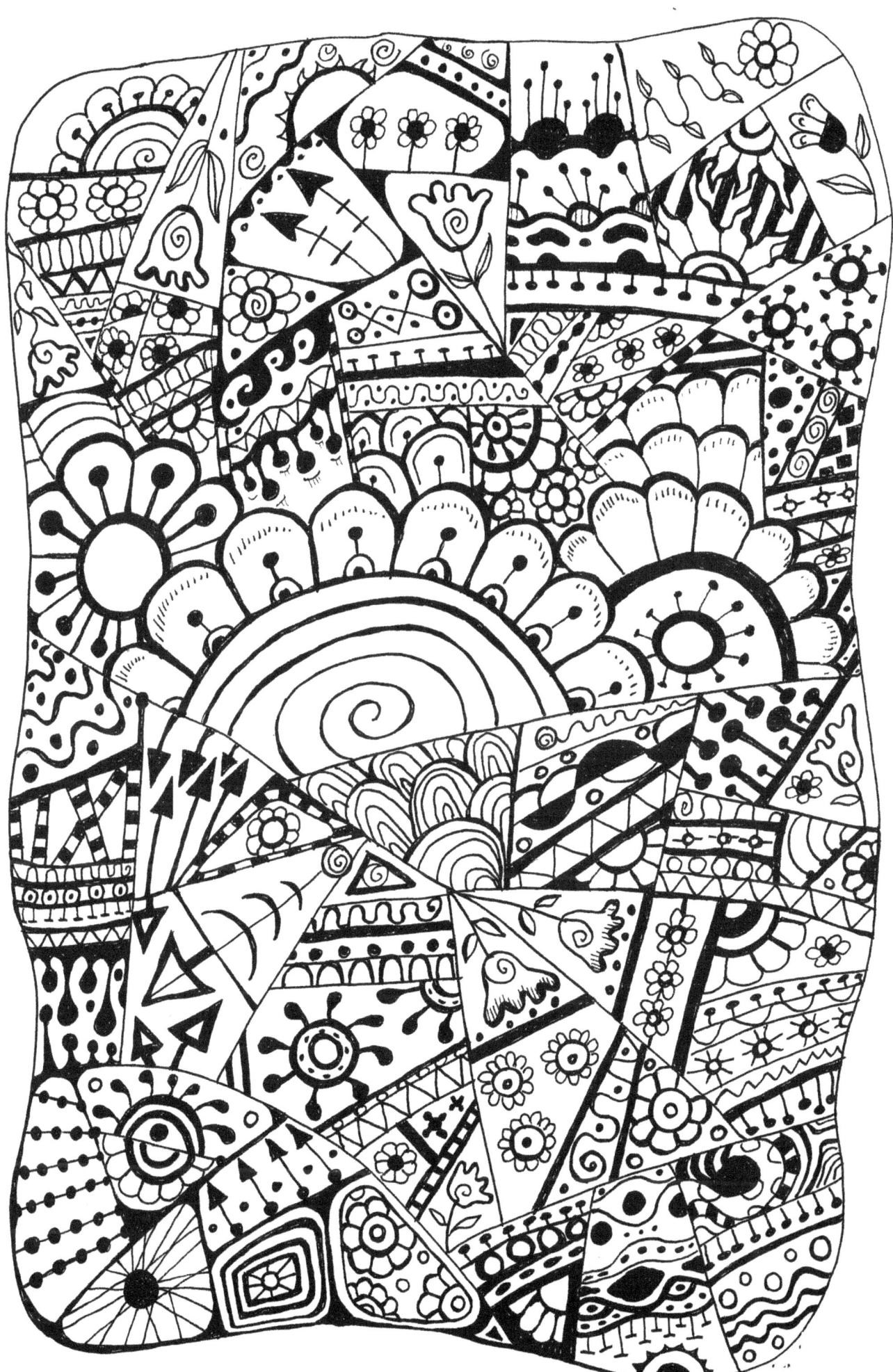

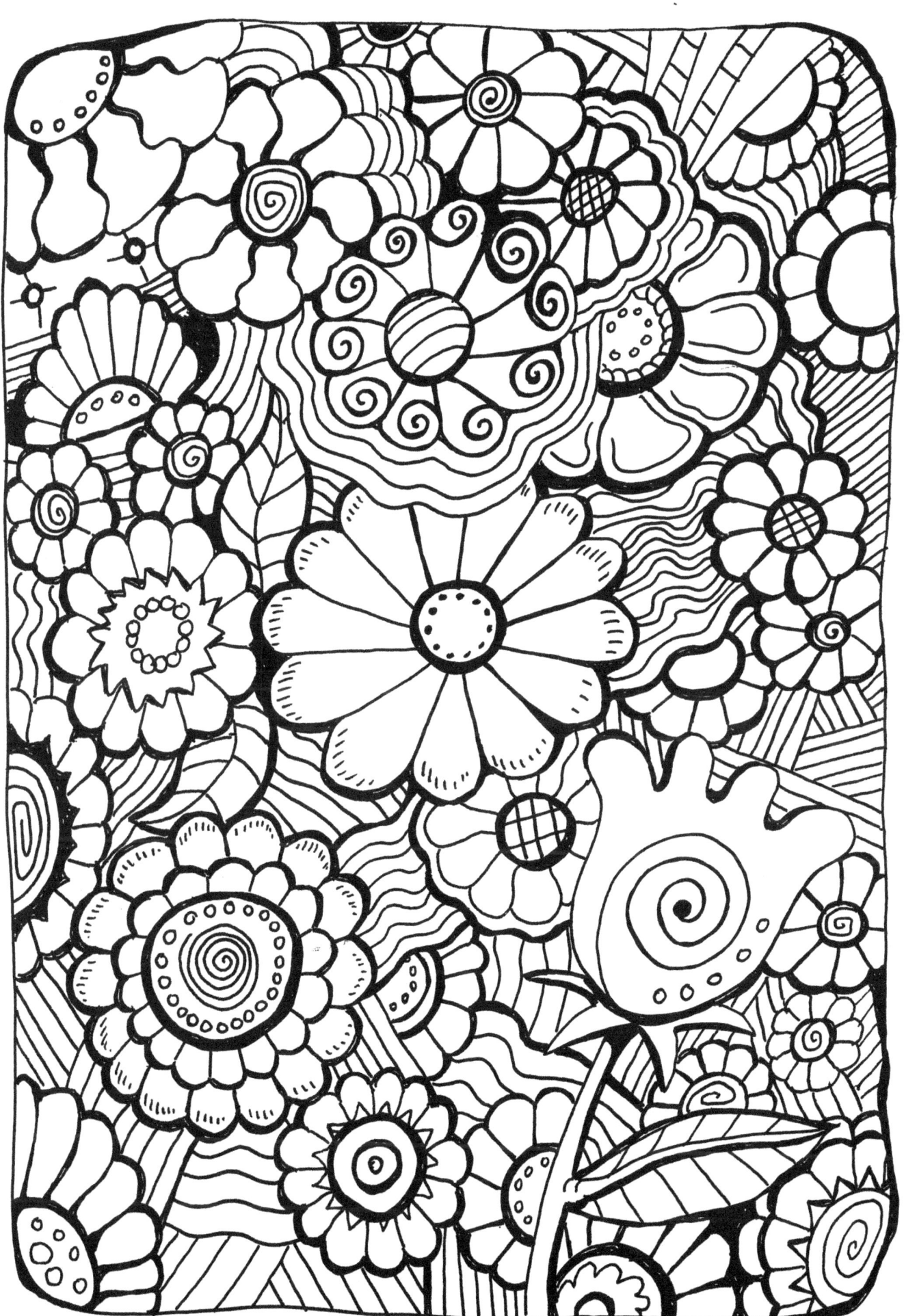

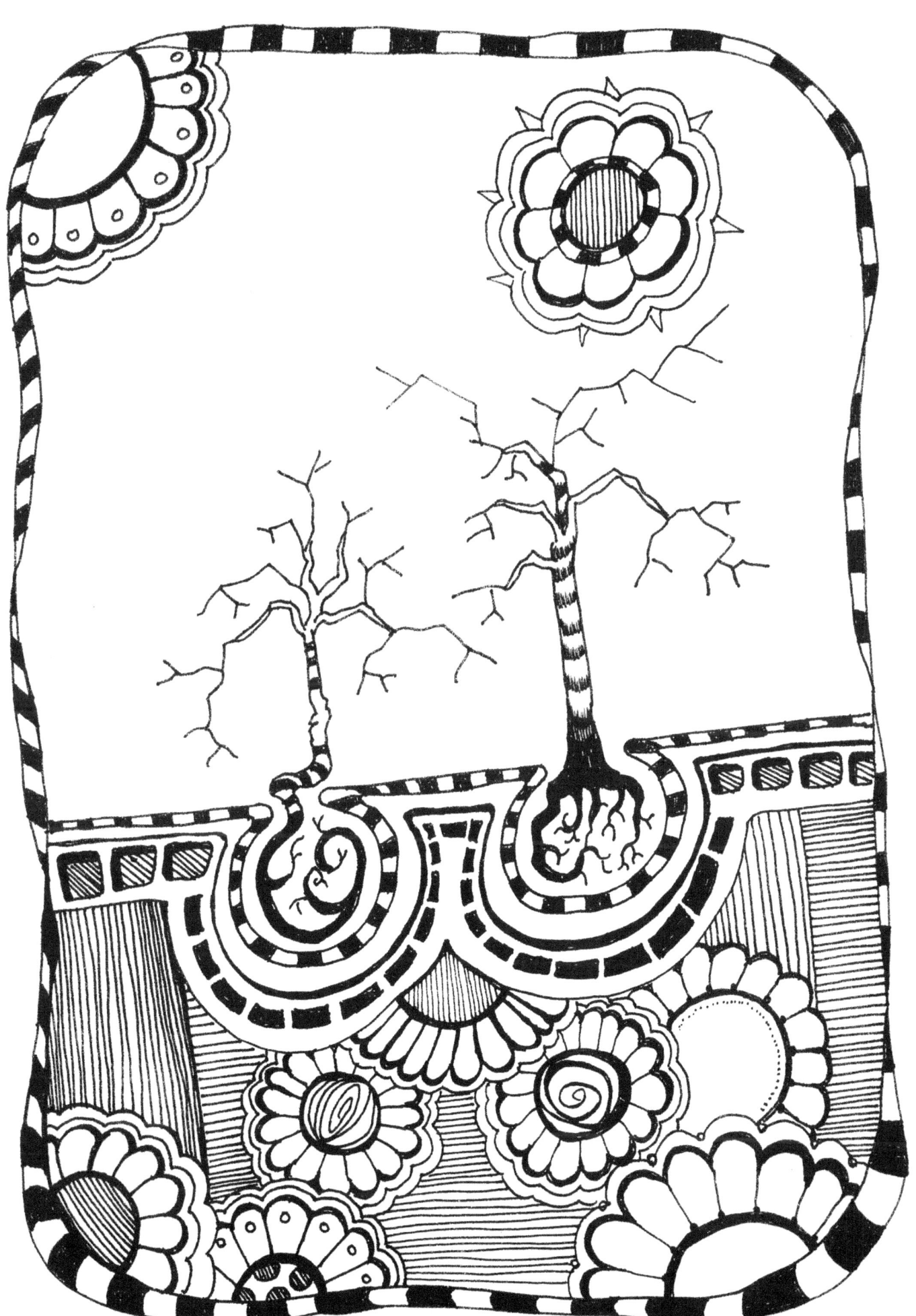

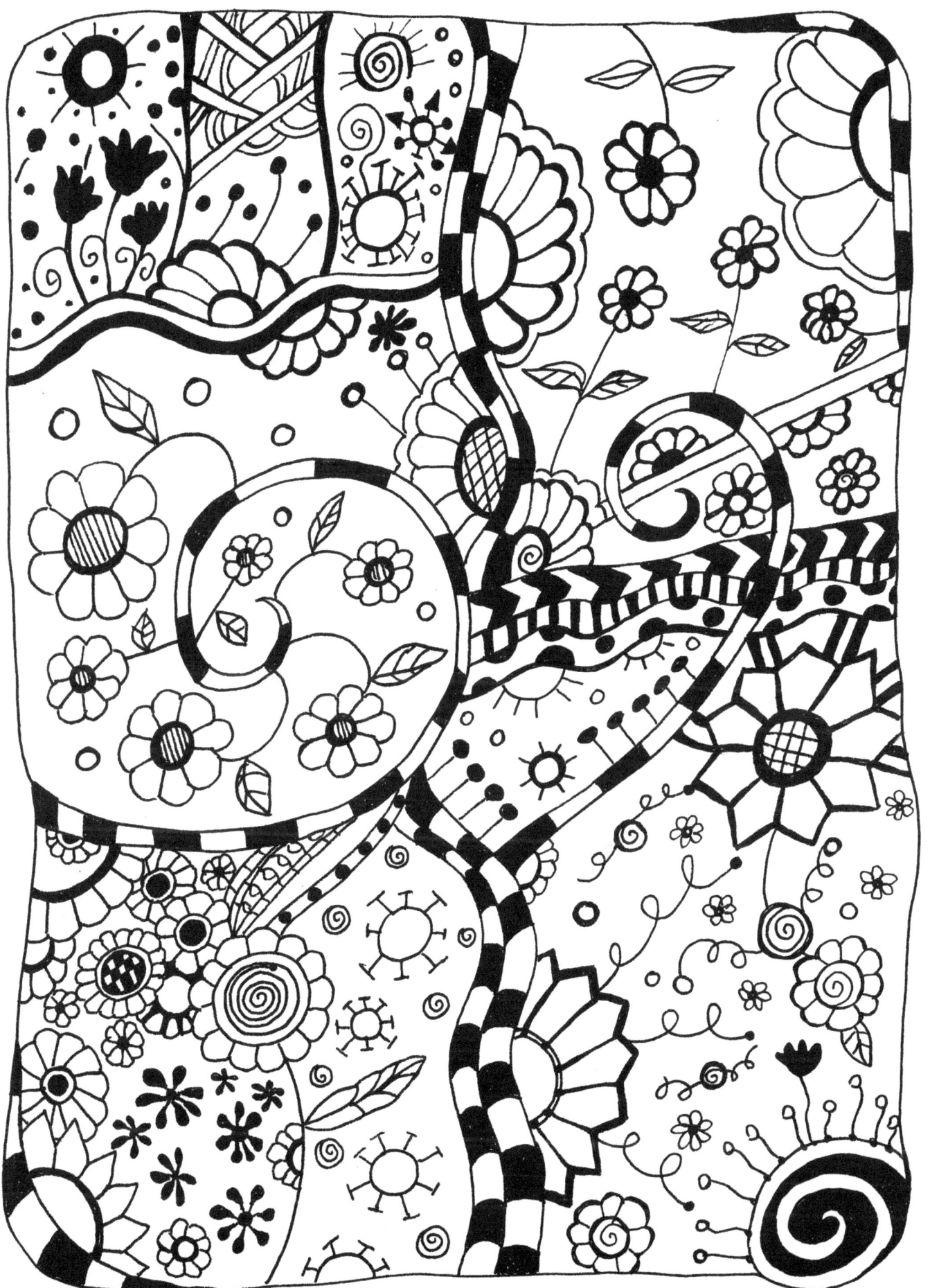

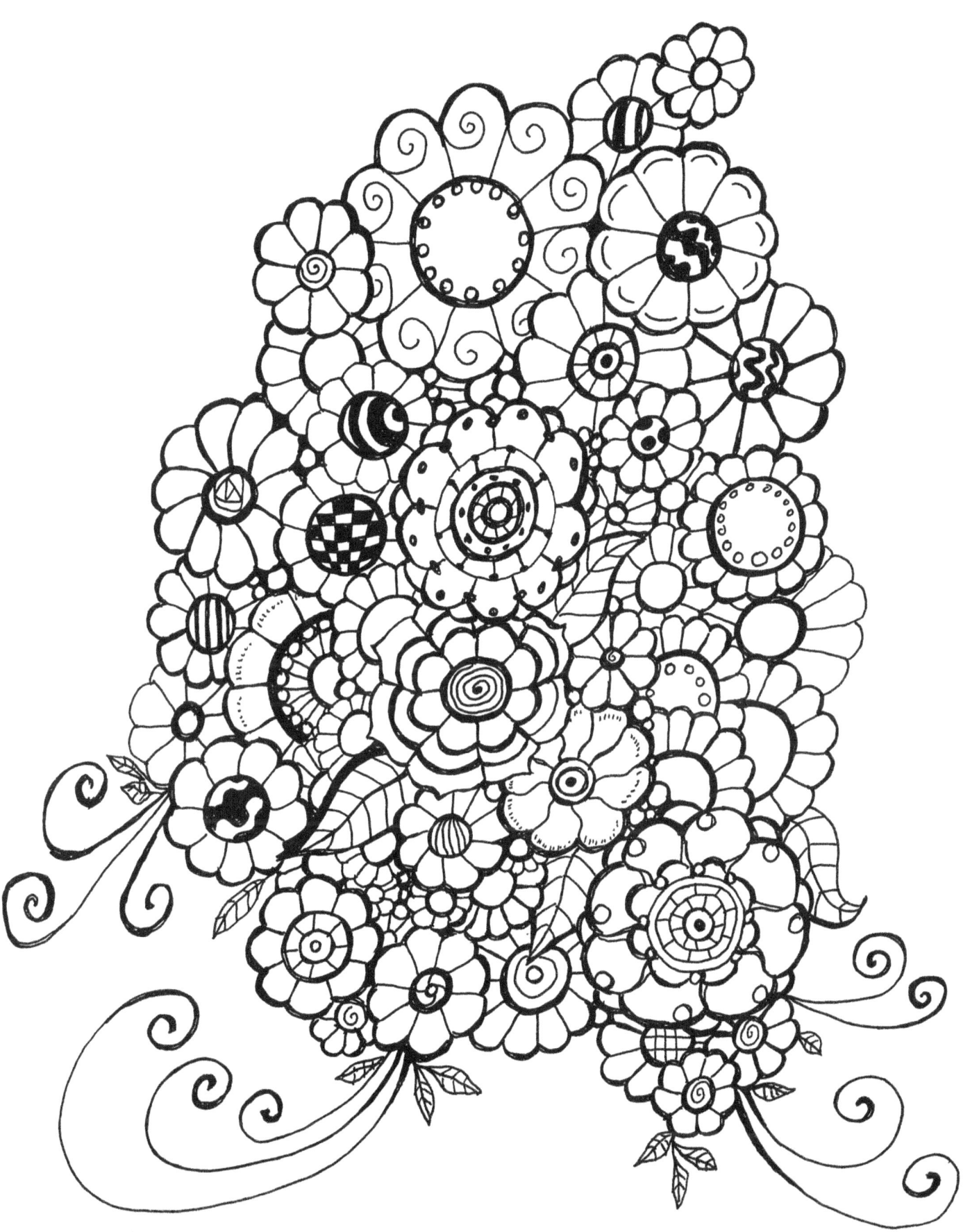

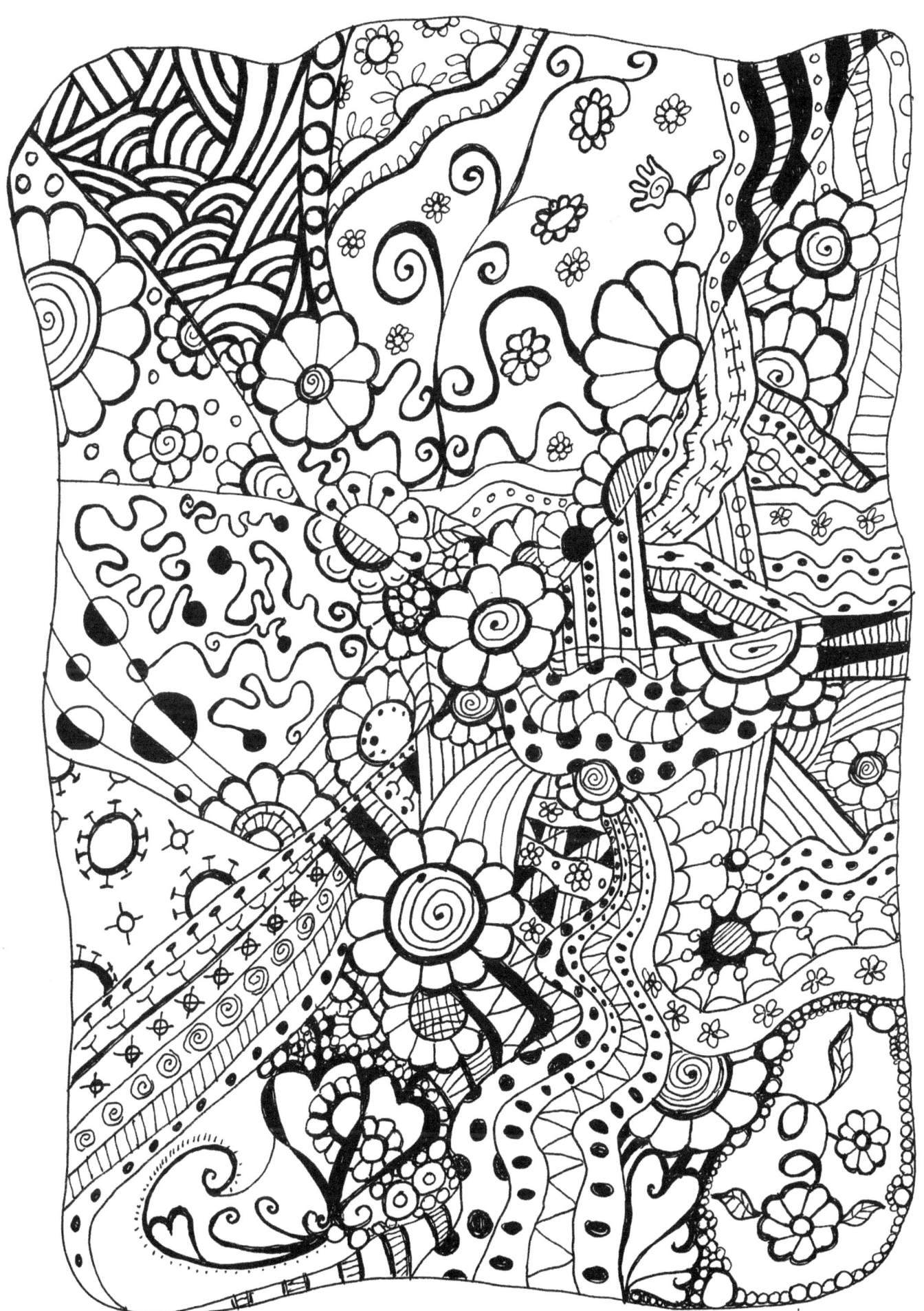

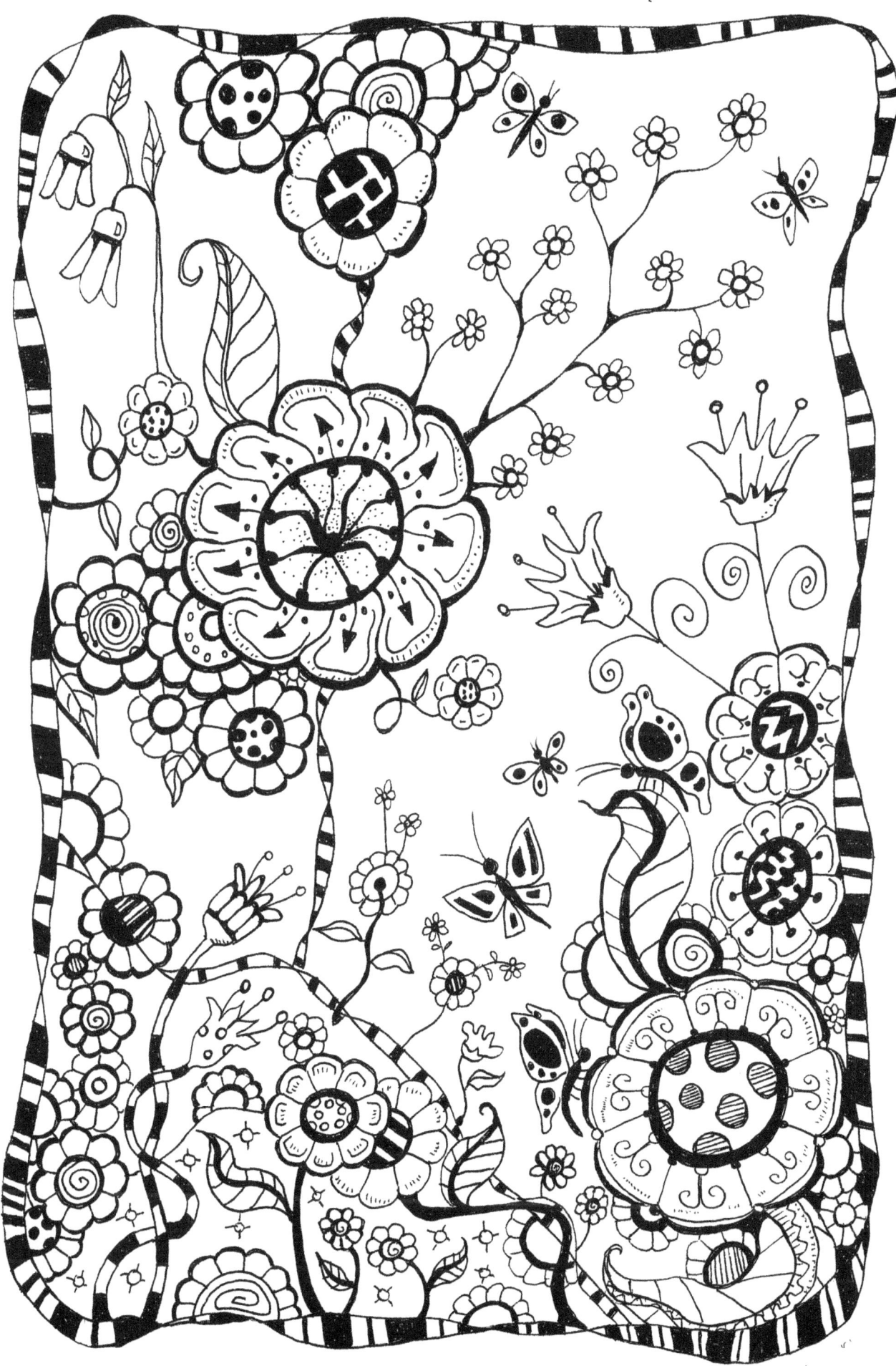

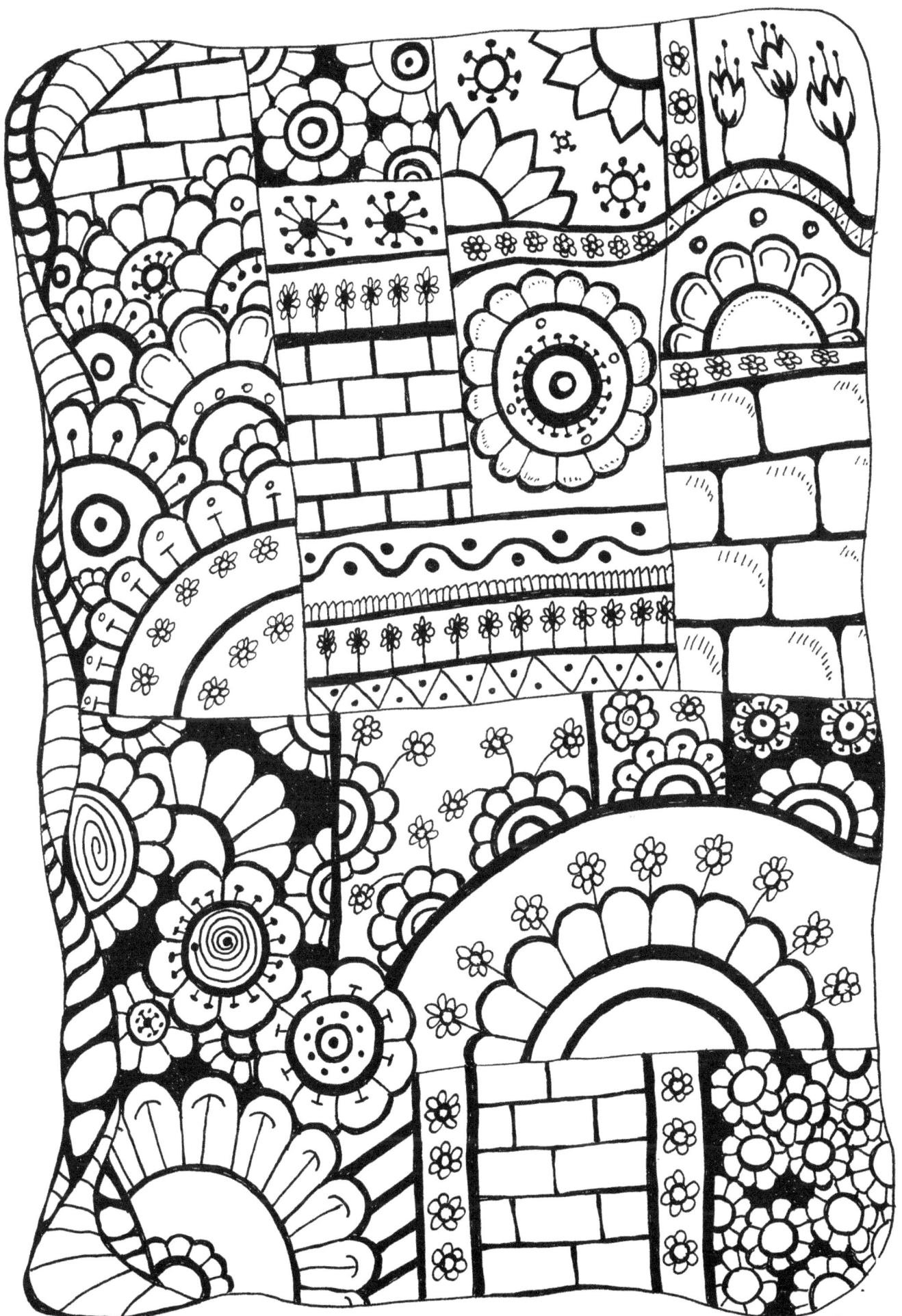

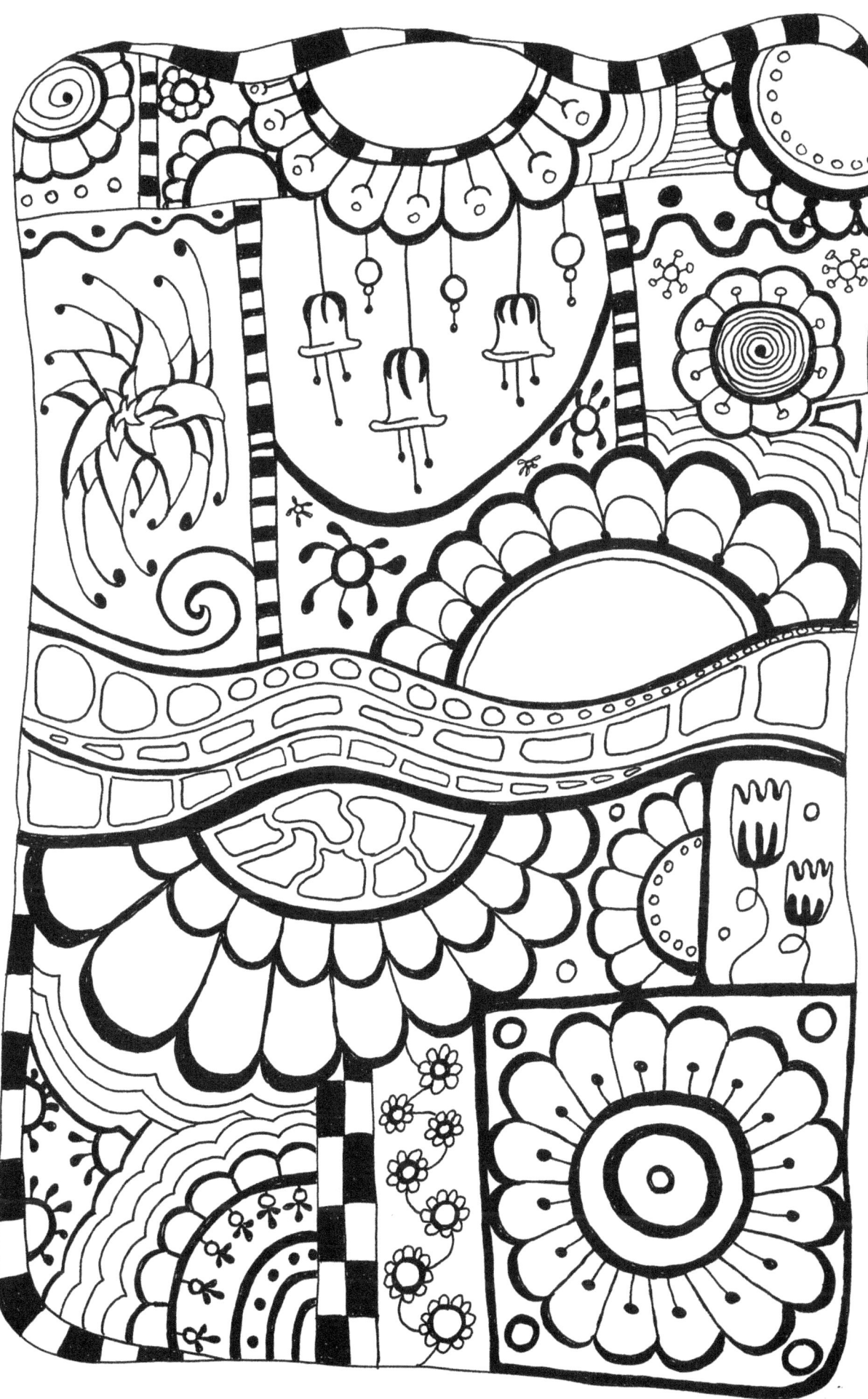

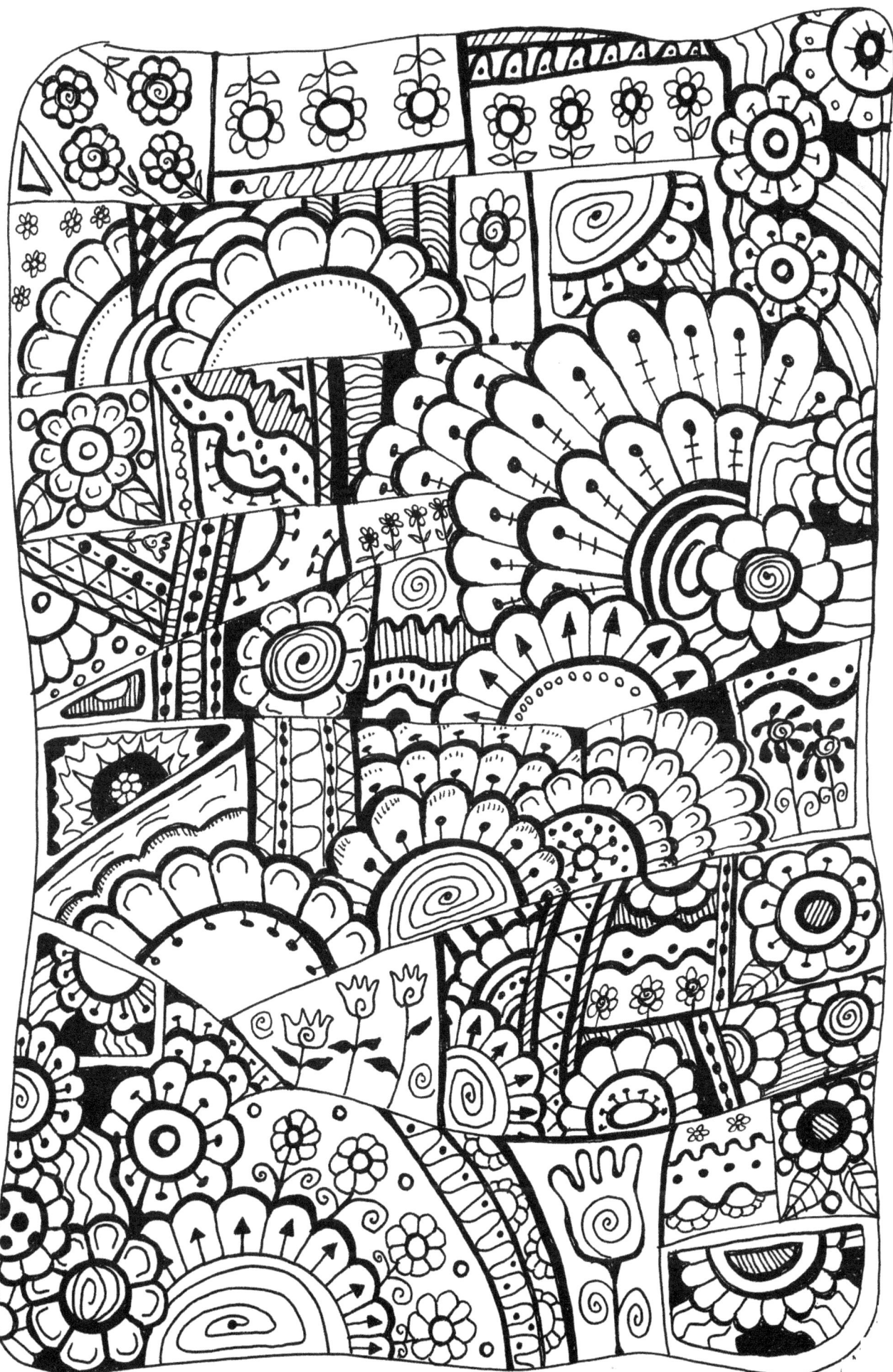

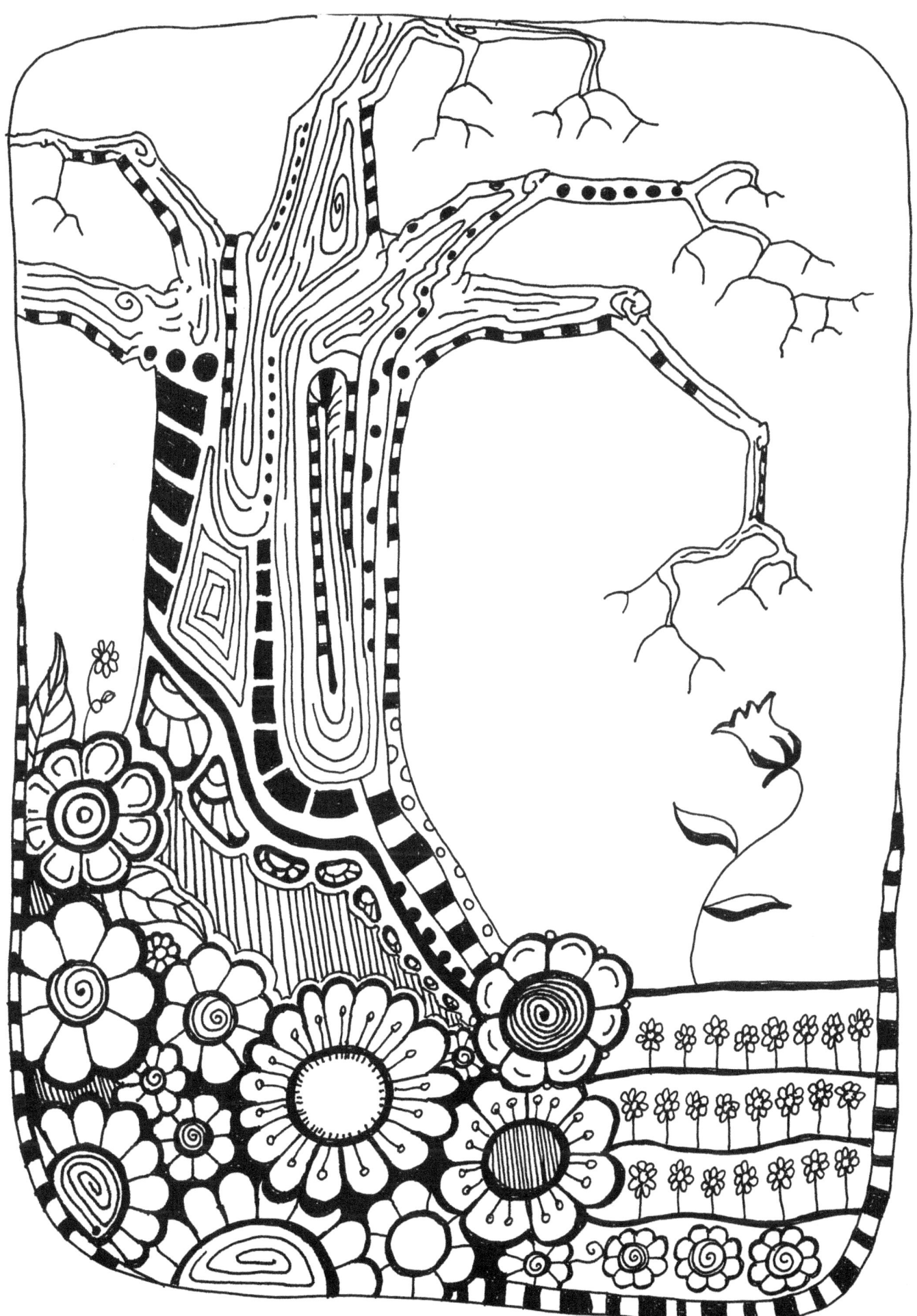

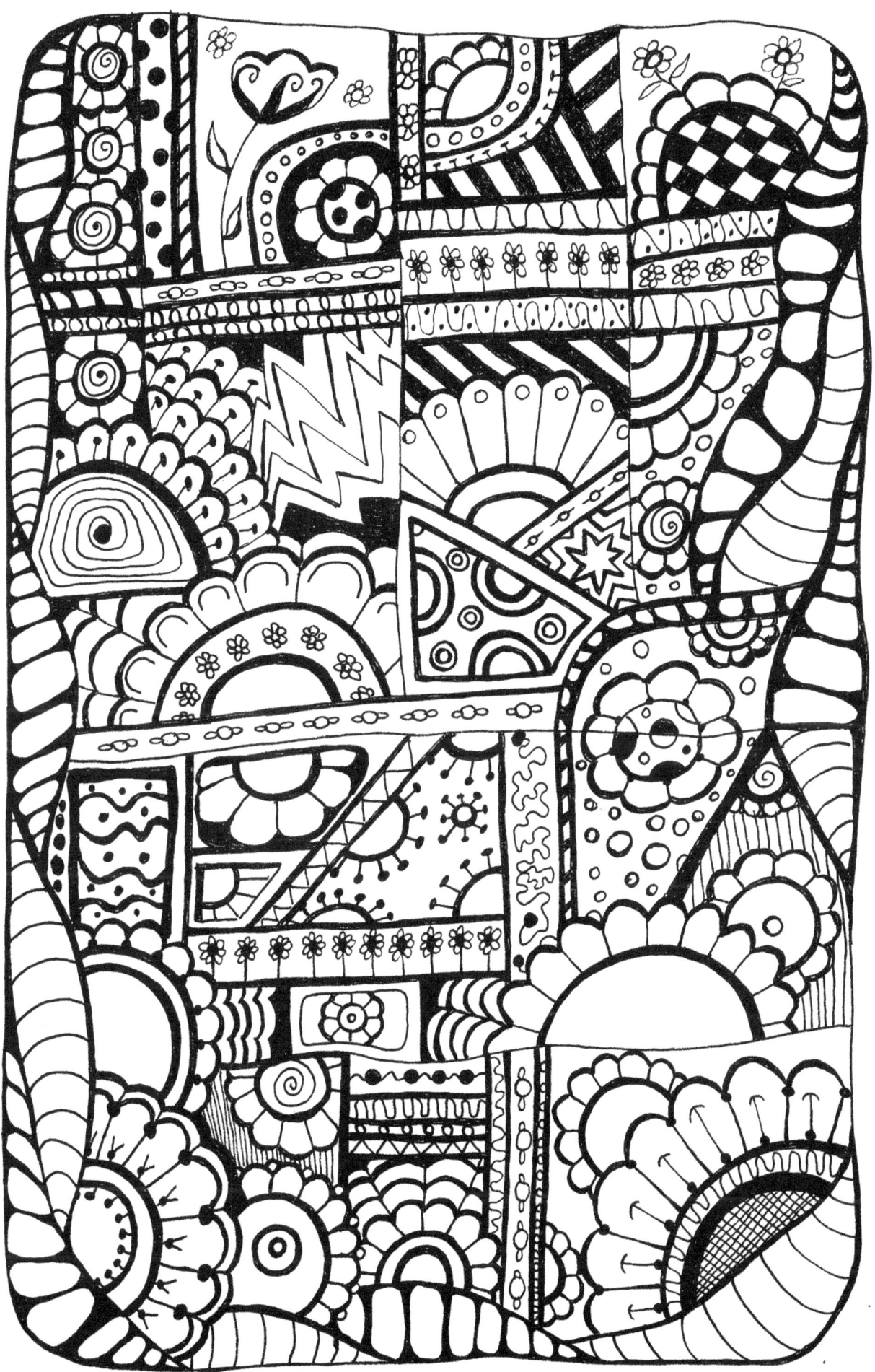

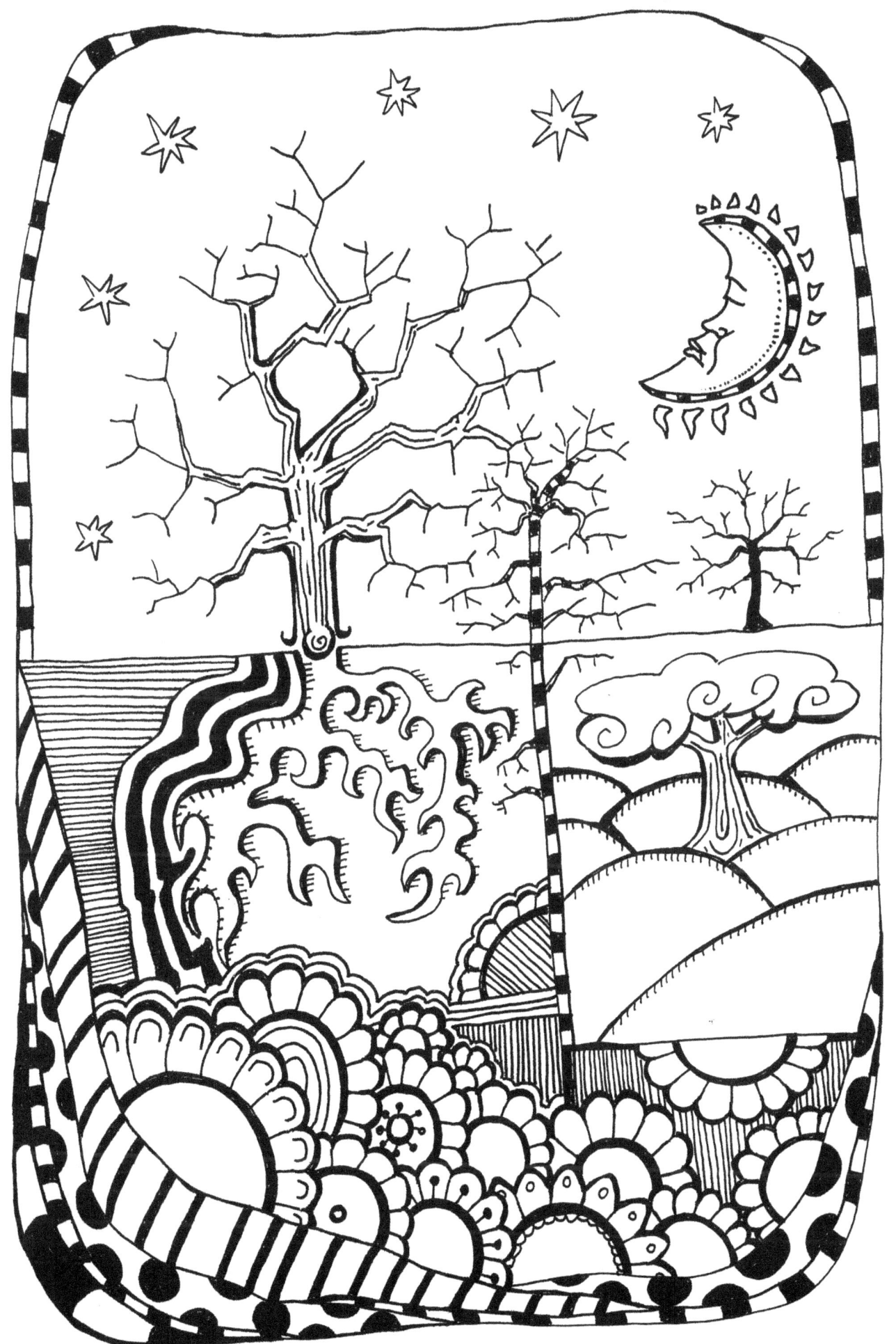

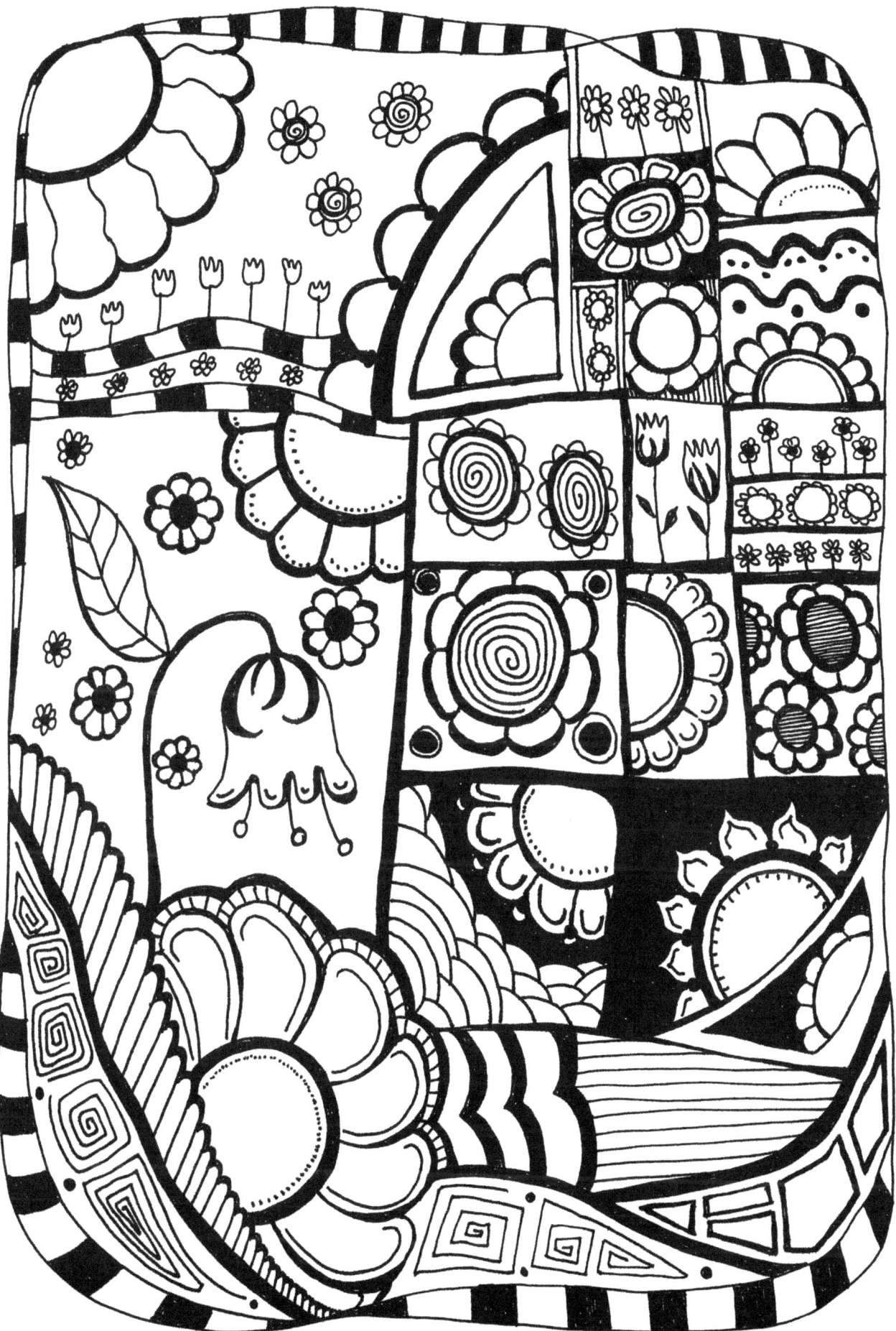

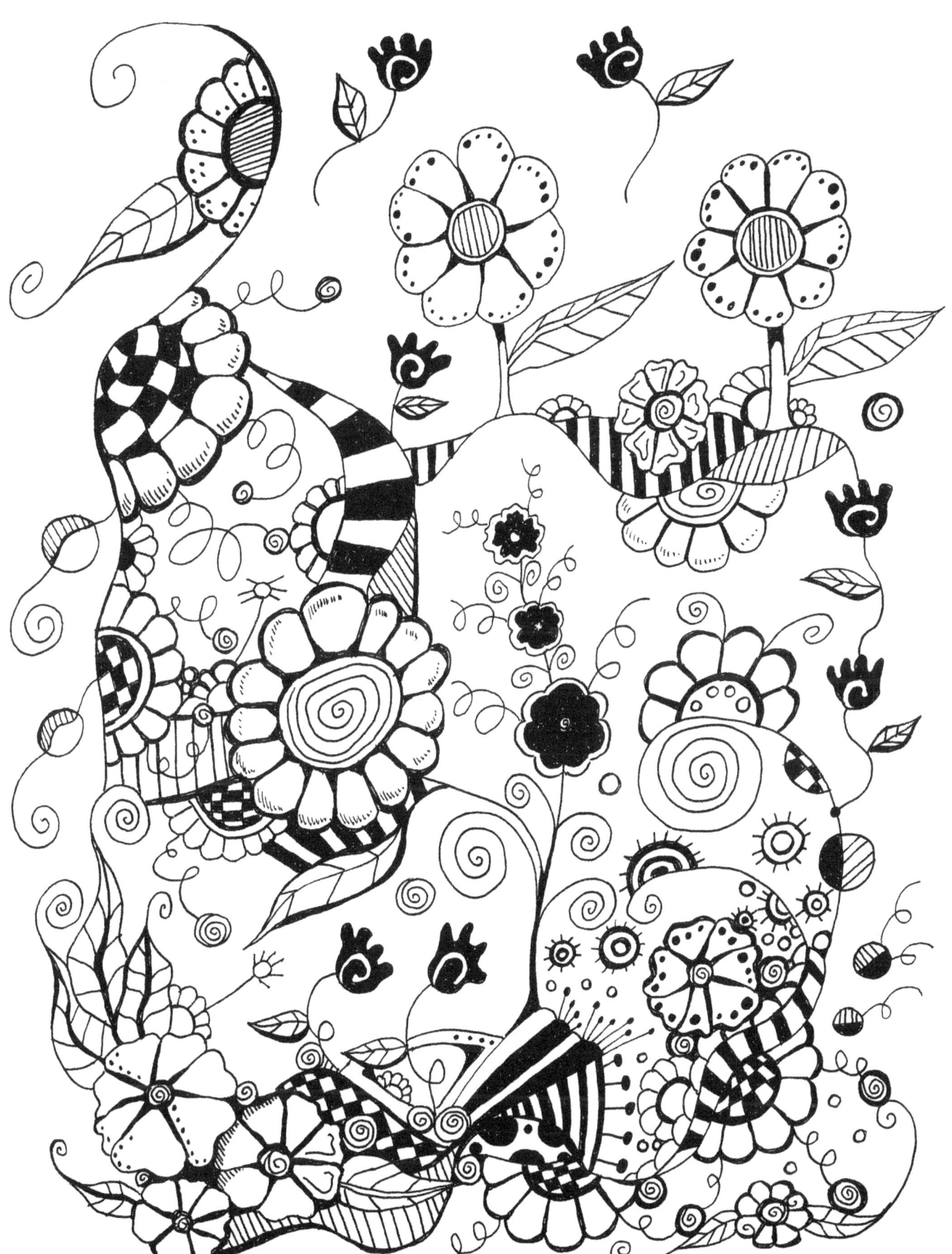

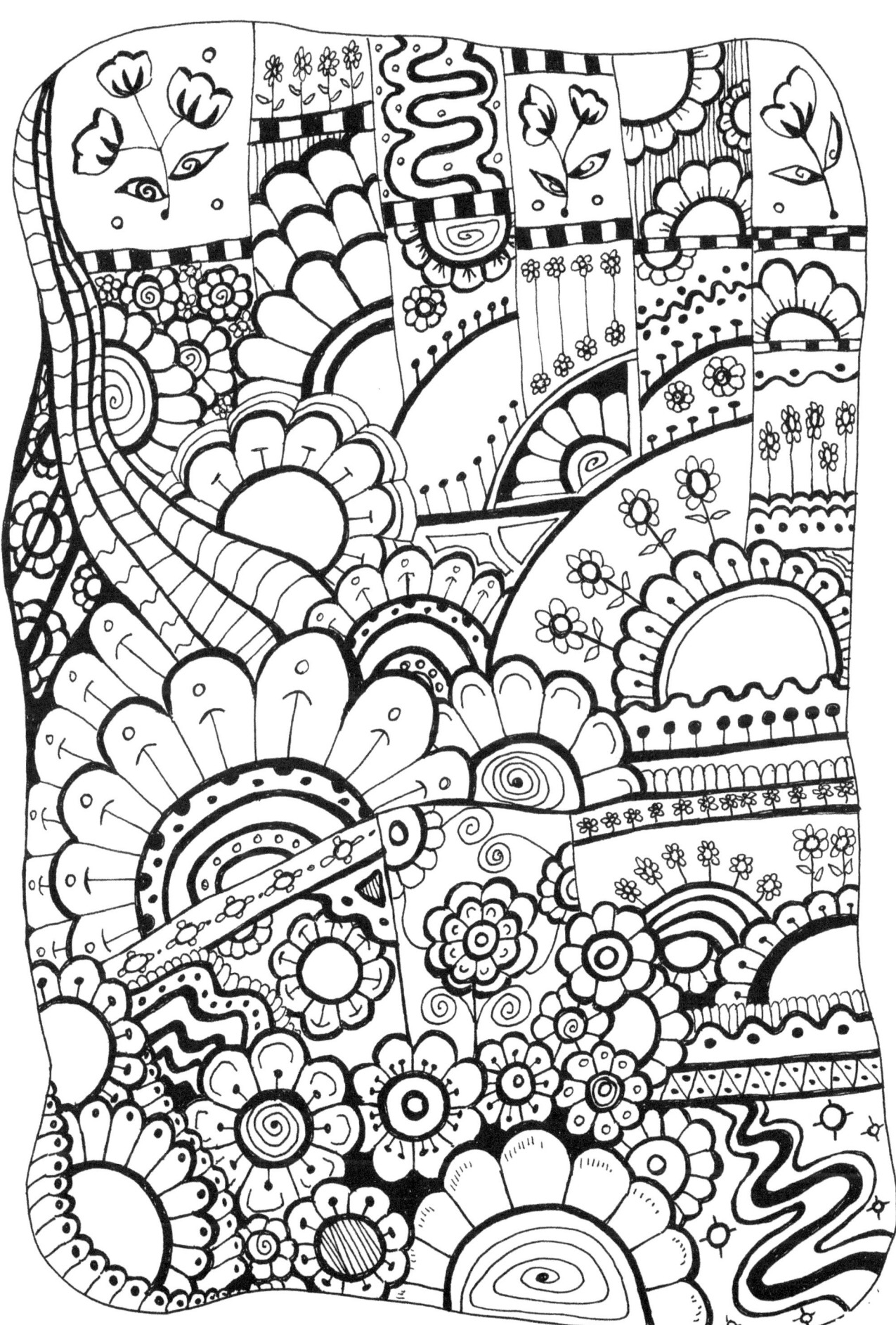

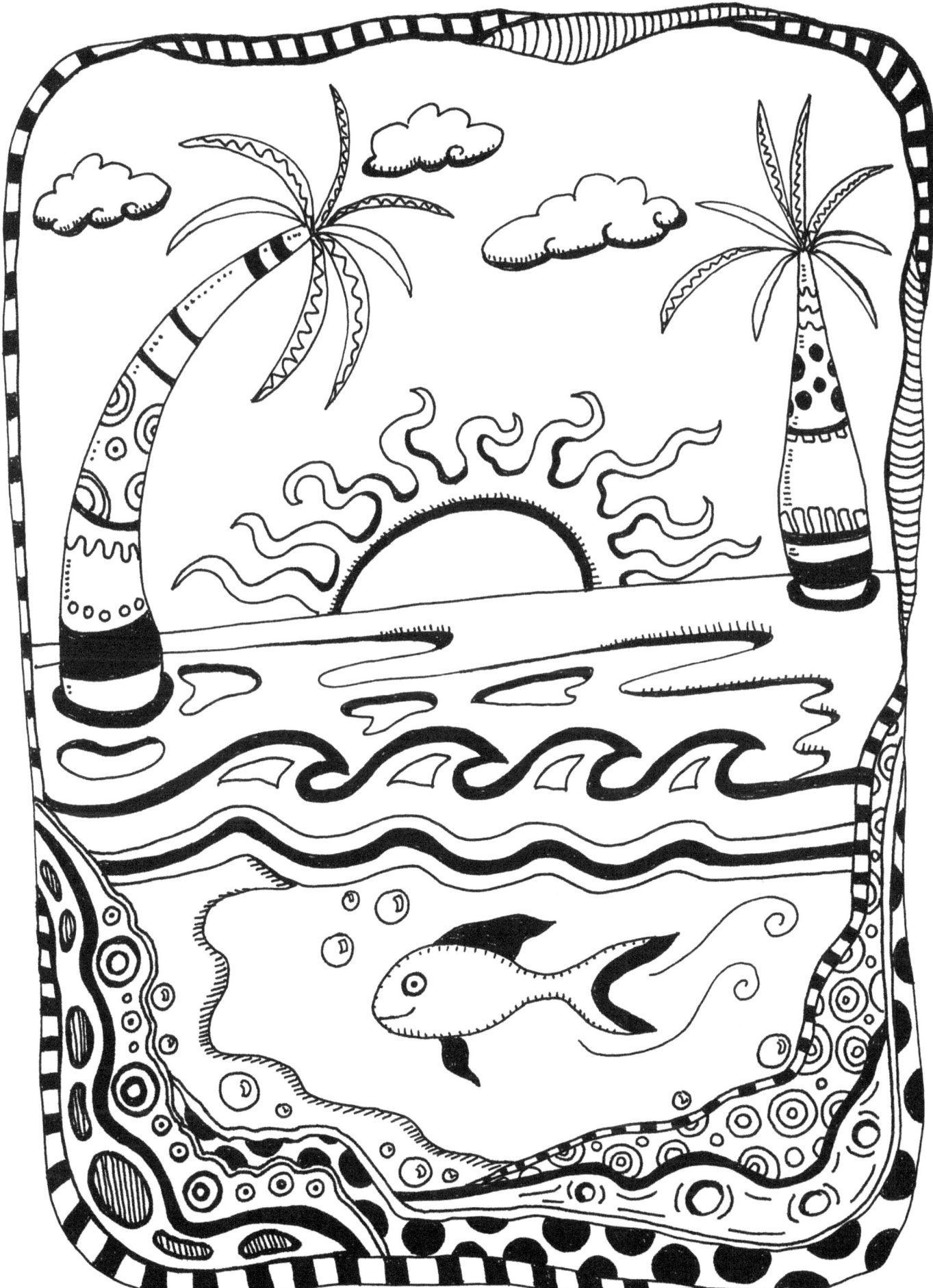

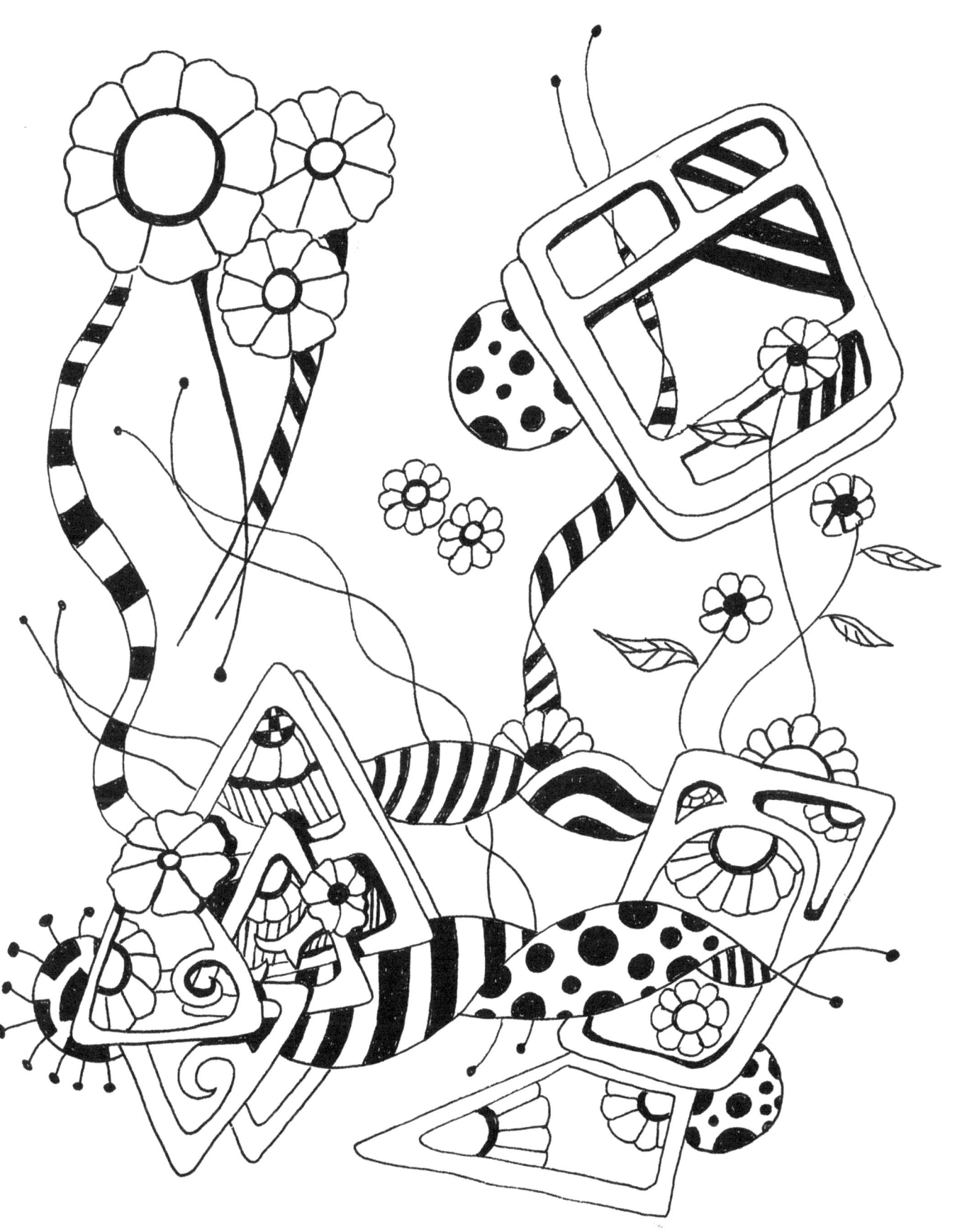

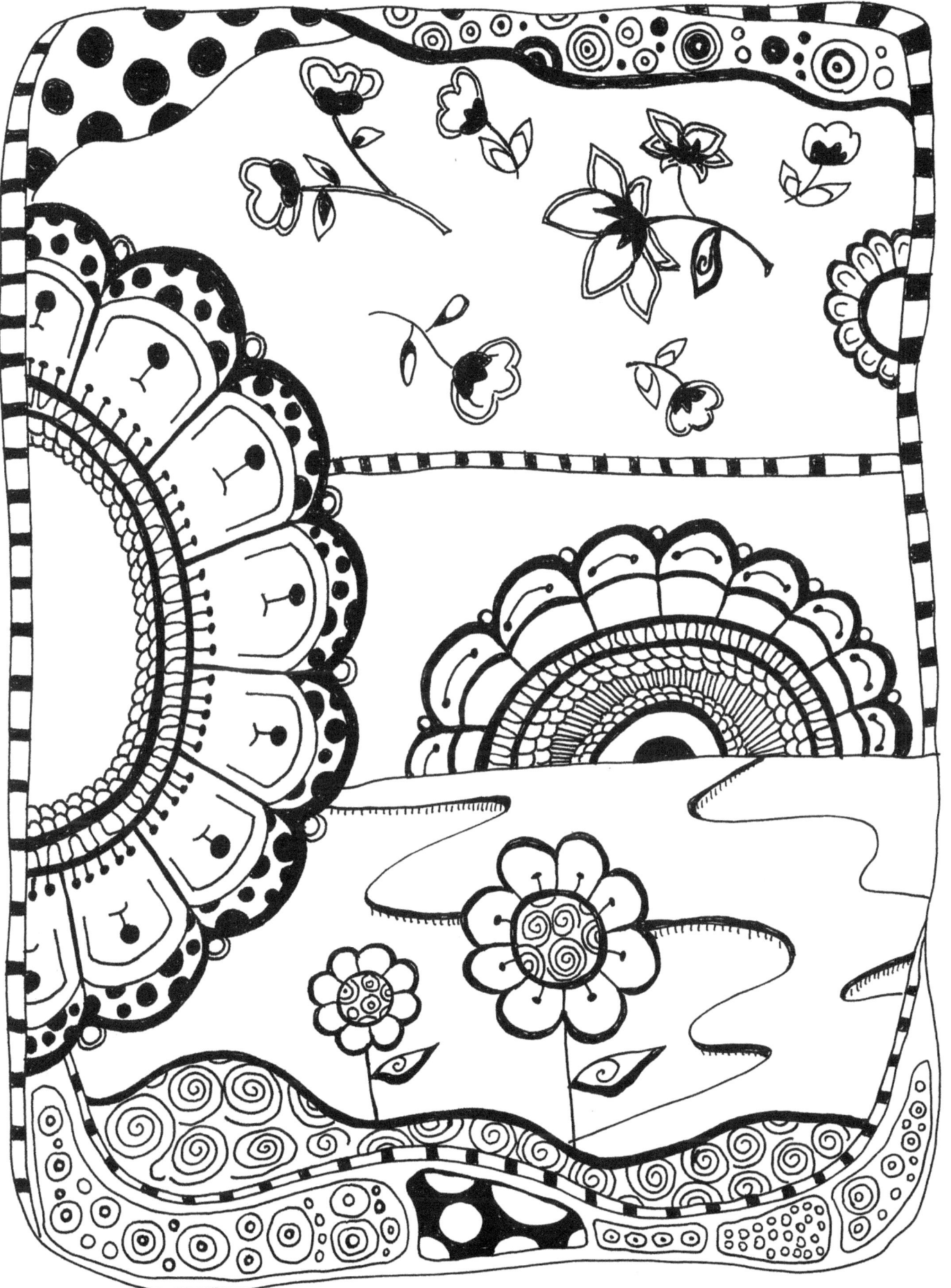

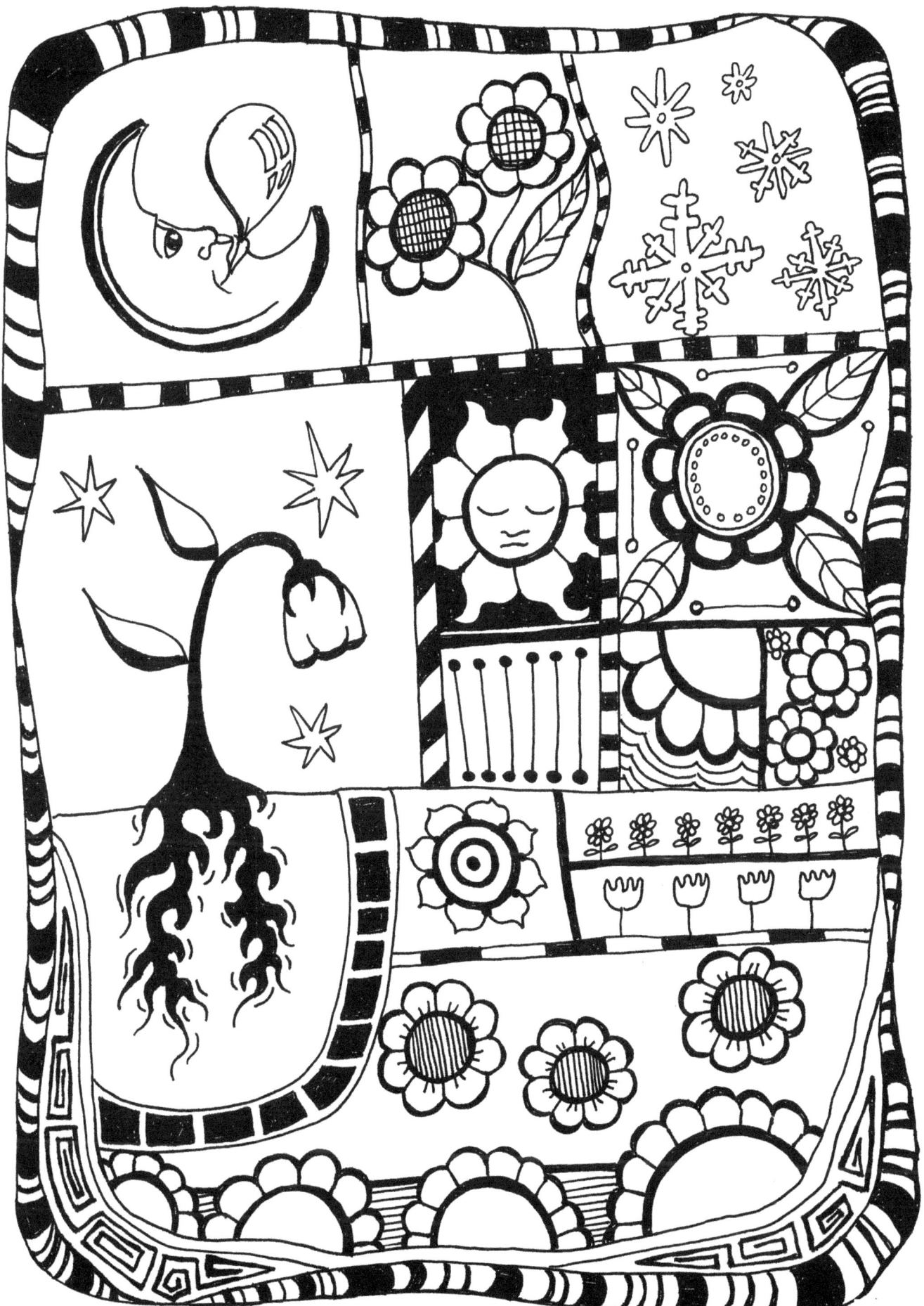

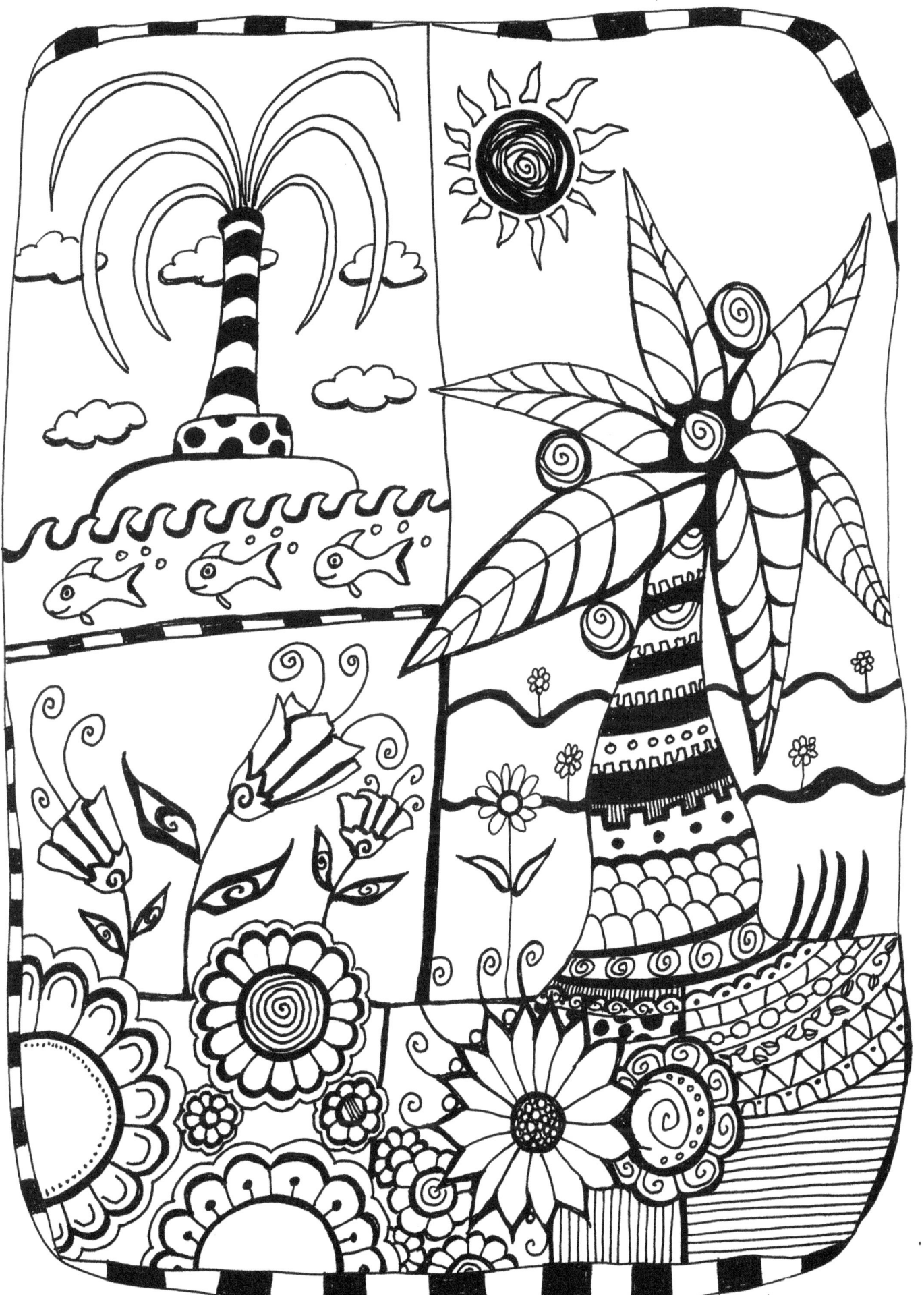

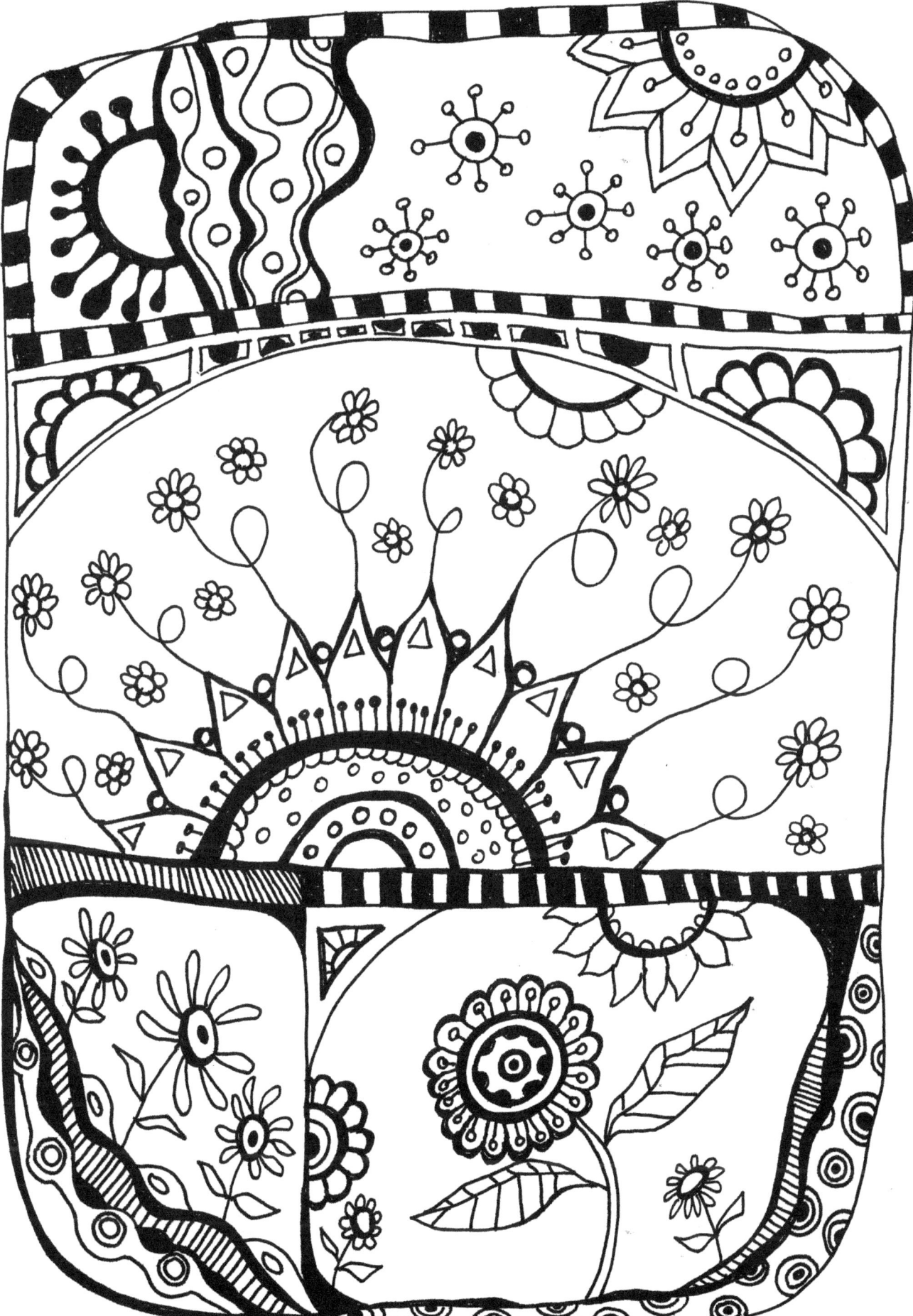

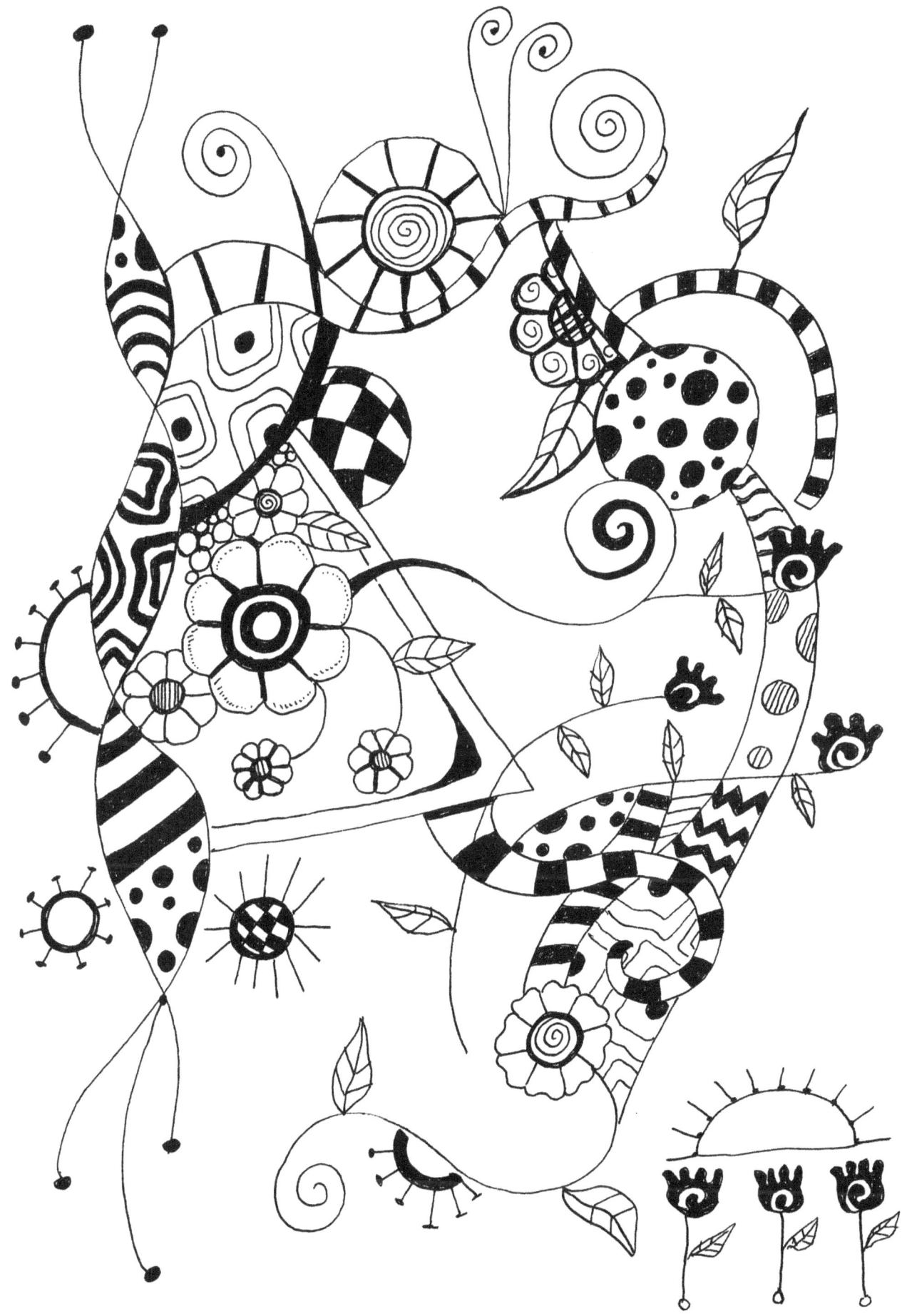

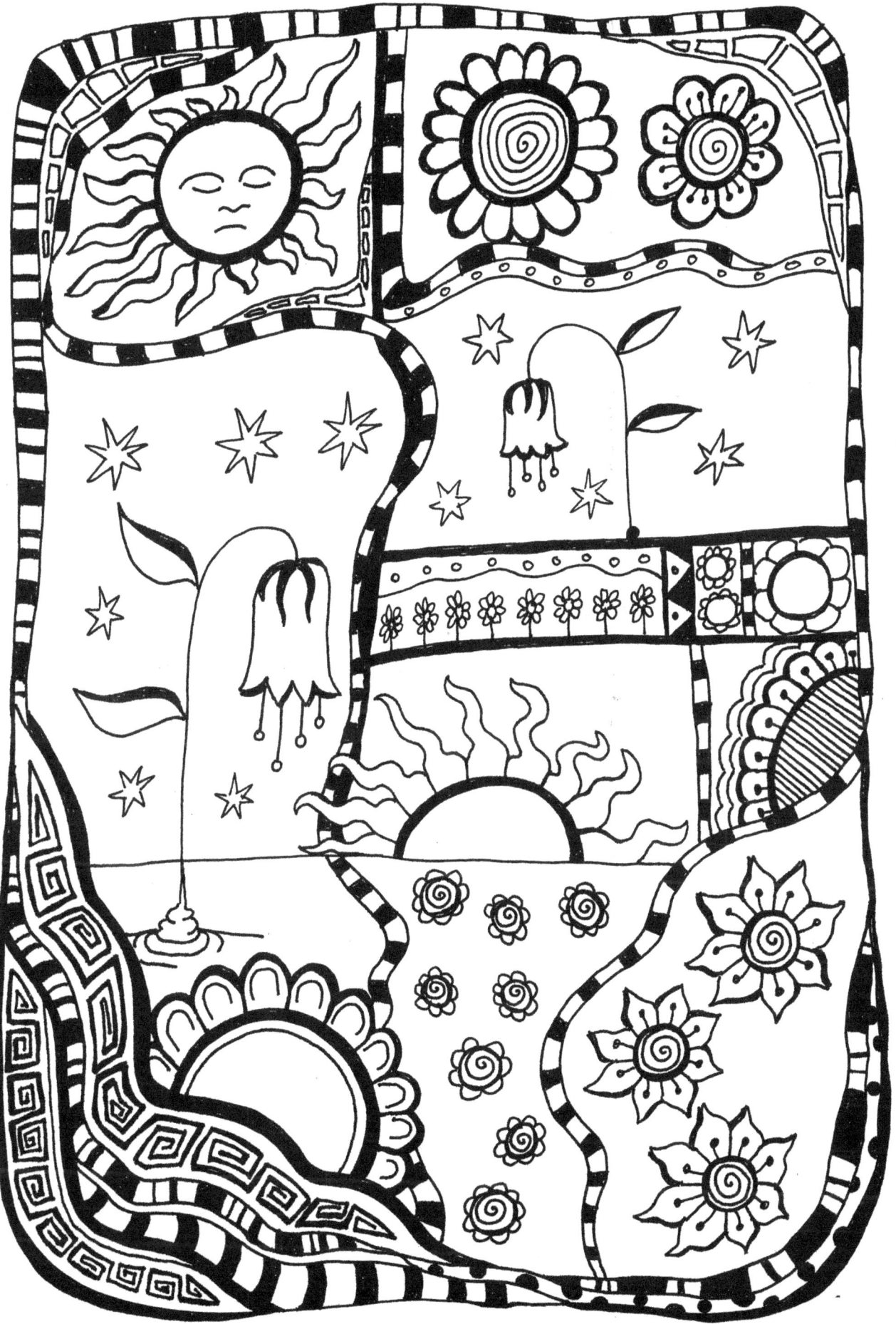

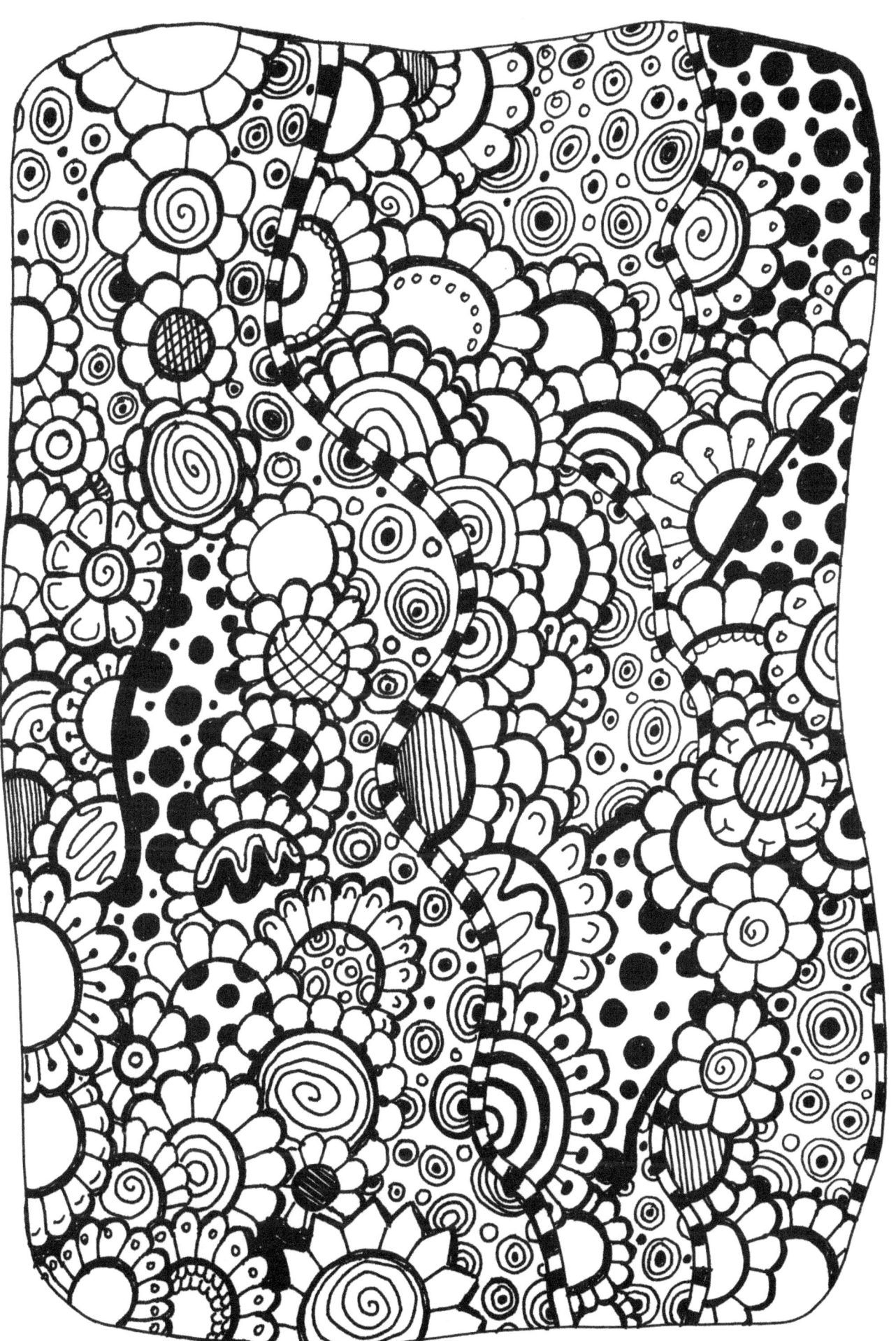

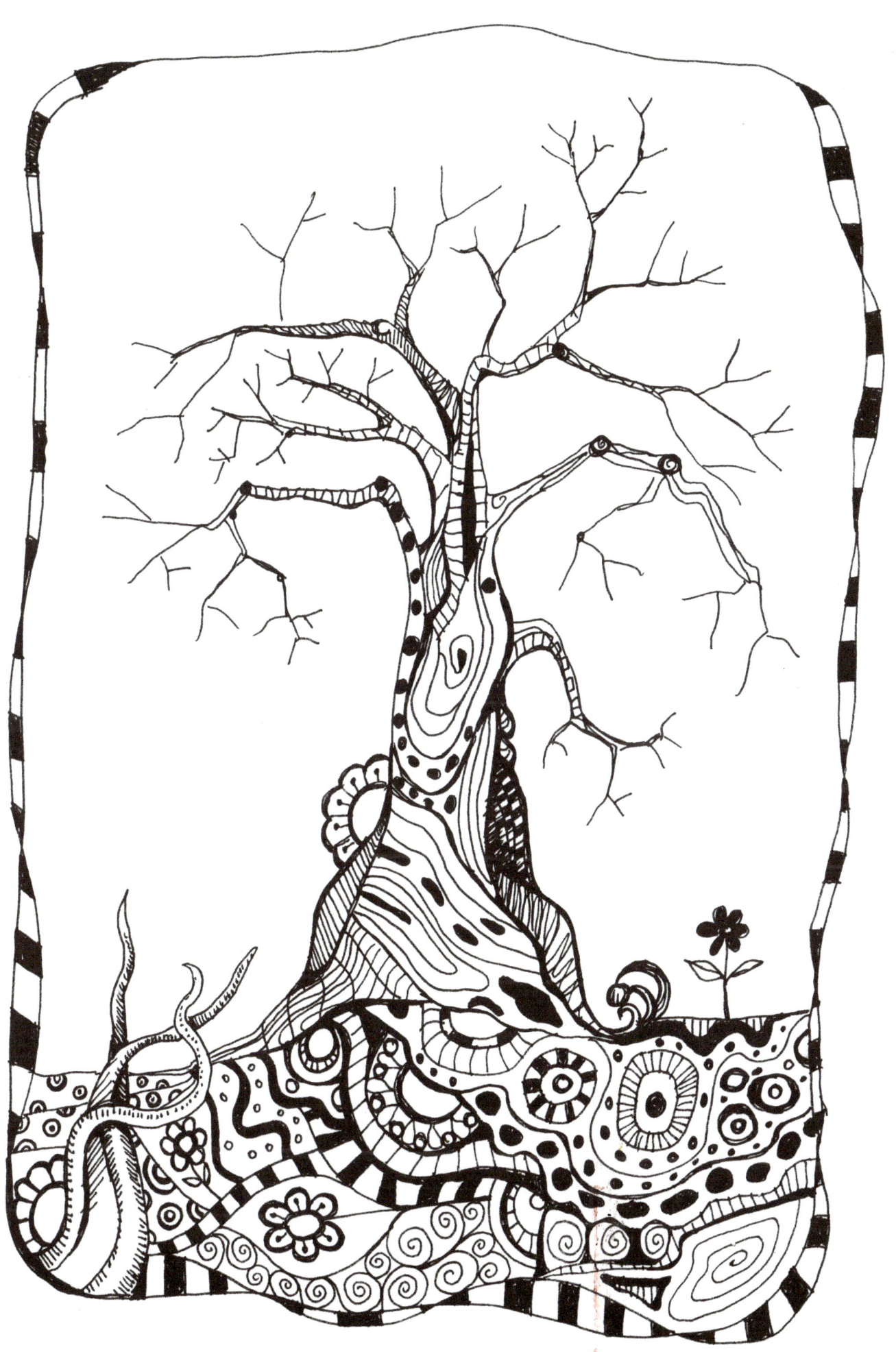

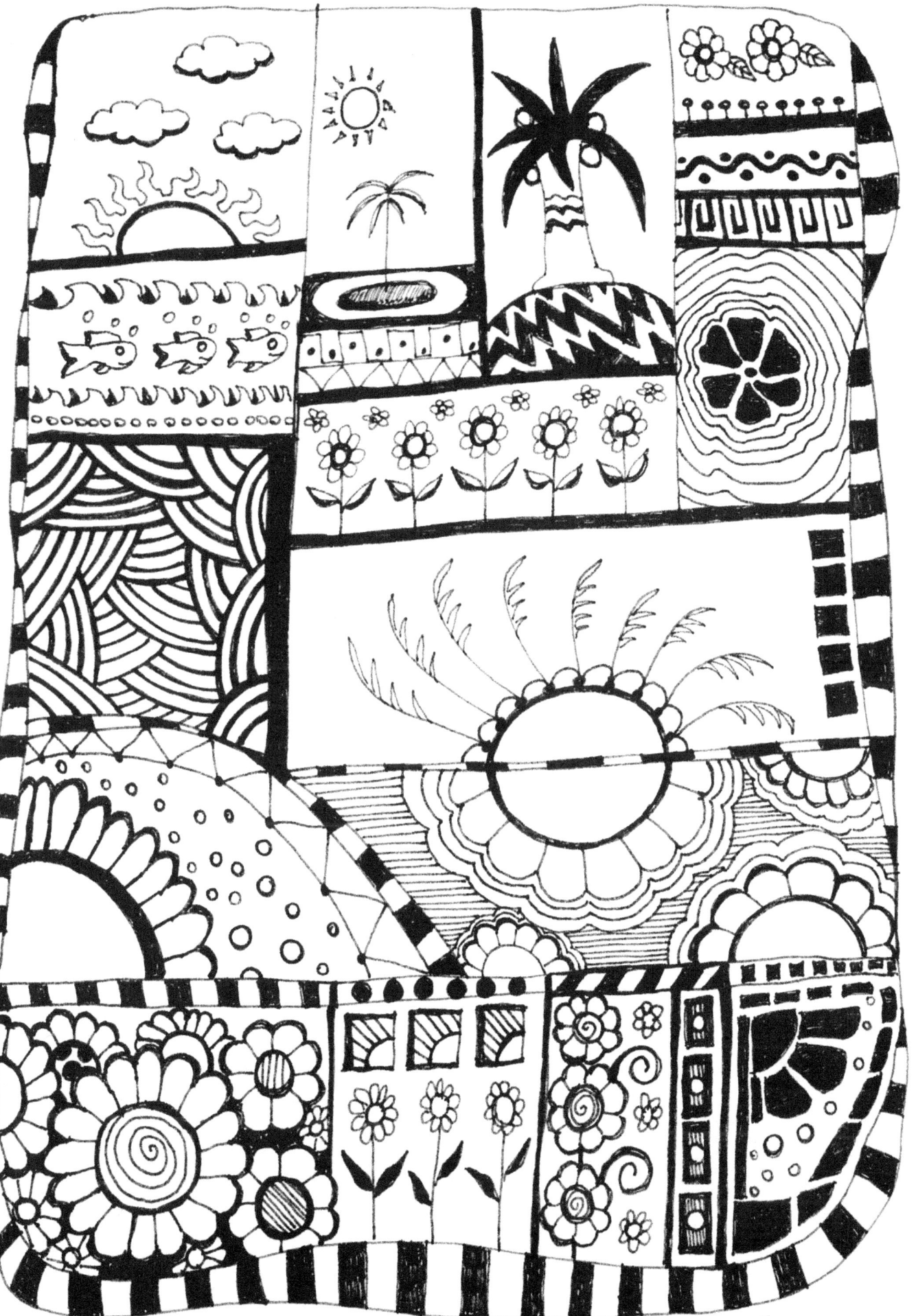

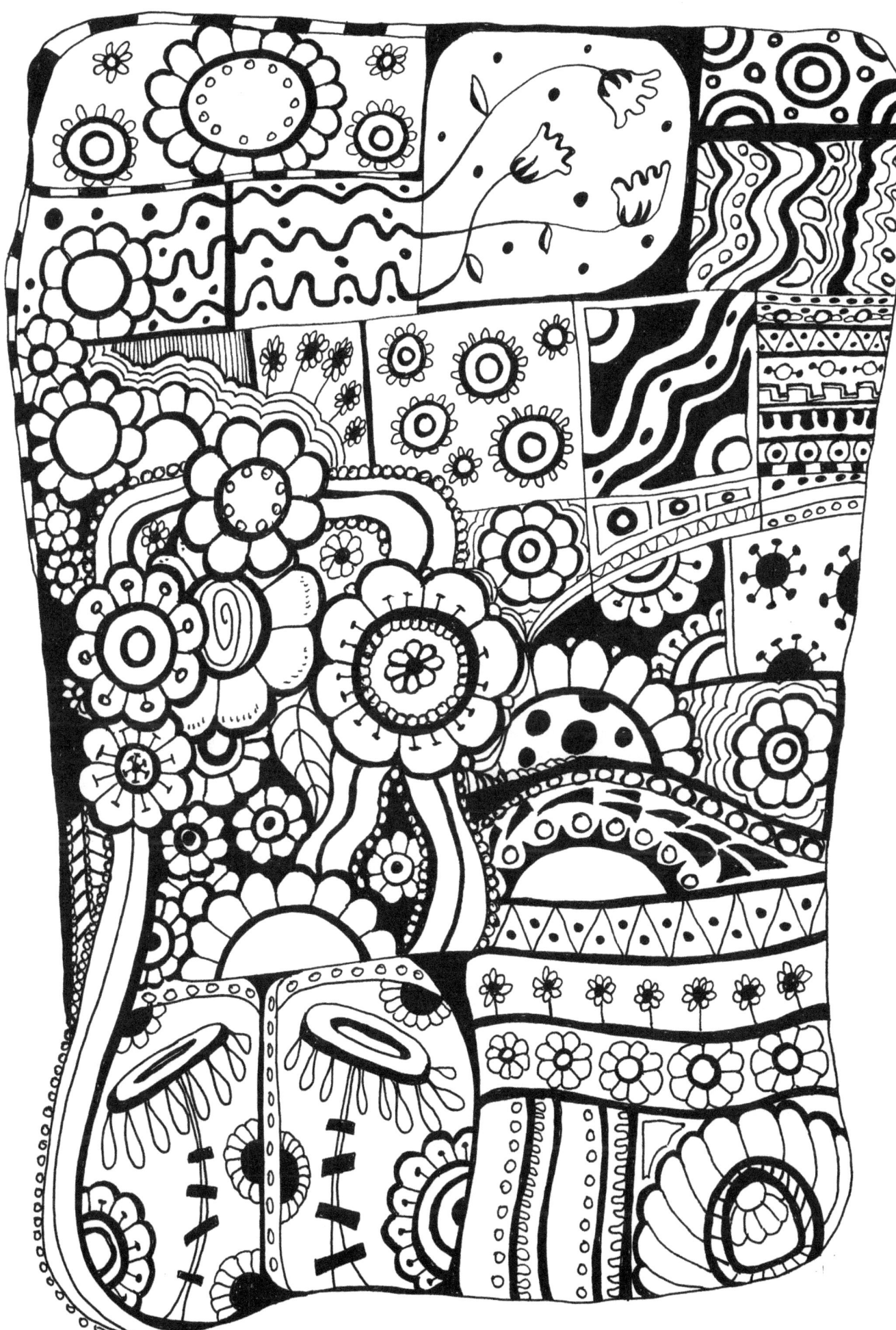

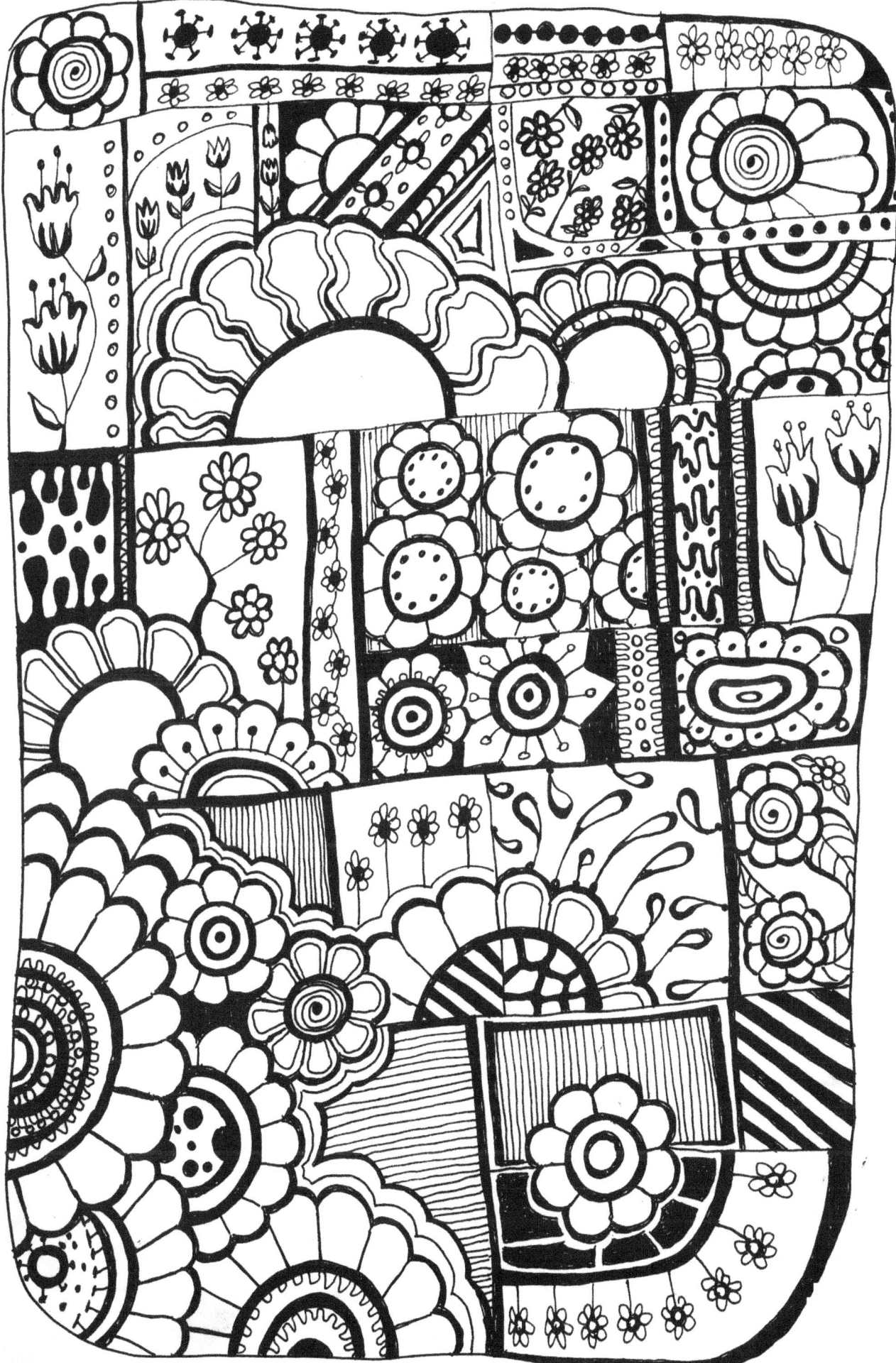